THE CAM SANTIAGU COMPANION

MW00897312

HIDDEN GEMS, BEST STOPS, AND TRAVEL TIPS

MICAH JEZRIEL

Table of Contents

1

Chapter 3. Navigating the Camino: Maps, Signs, and Apps

Reading Camino Waymarks and Signs

Using Apps and GPS for Navigation

Finding Your Way in Remote Areas

Tips for Staying Safe on the Trail

Chapter 4. Accommodation on the Camino

Types of Accommodation: Hostels, Albergues, and Hotels

Top-Rated Albergues to Stay In

Booking Tips and Reservations

Budget-Friendly Lodging Options

Sleeping Tips for Shared Spaces

Chapter 5. Camino Diet: Eating Well on the Trail

Traditional Spanish Cuisine to Try

Where to Find the Best Pilgrim Menus

Budget Tips for Food and Drink

Healthy Snacks for Energy and Stamina

Dietary Considerations: Vegetarian, Vegan, and Gluten-Free Options

Chapter 6. Hidden Gems Along the Camino de Santiago

Must-See Villages and Towns Off the Beaten Path

Scenic Detours and Viewpoints

Local Traditions and Festivals Worth Visiting

Unique Stops for Nature Lovers

Artistic and Historical Sights Beyond the Main Route

Chapter 7. Essential Stops on the Camino: Landmarks and Icons

Starting Point: Saint-Jean-Pied-de-Port

Must-Visit Churches and Cathedrals

Famous Bridges and Historic Sites

Natural Wonders: Forests, Rivers, and Mountains

Santiago de Compostela: The End of the Journey

Chapter 8. Pilgrim Etiquette and Camino Culture

Camino Customs and Local Traditions

Respecting Fellow Pilgrims and Locals

Understanding the Spirit of the Camino

Building Connections: Meeting Fellow Travelers

Giving Back to the Camino Community

Chapter 9. Challenges and Rewards of the Camino

Physical Challenges: Terrain, Weather, and Fatigue

Mental and Emotional Challenges

How to Overcome the "Camino Wall"

The Rewards of Completing the Camino

Lessons Learned on the Camino

Chapter 10. Health and Safety on the Camino

Introduction to the Camino de Santiago

The Camino de Santiago, often called "The Way of Saint James," has been a journey of faith, self-discovery, and endurance for centuries. Whether it's the historical appeal, spiritual resonance, or sense of adventure that draws people, walking the Camino offers more than a physical trek; it's an experience that intertwines with one's personal growth, cultural appreciation, and connection to history. This book, The Camino de Santiago Companion: Hidden Gems, Best Stops, and Travel Tips, is designed to be your guide through the journey, providing insights into the best routes, must-see stops, practical tips, and much more.

The Historical and Spiritual Roots of the Camino

The roots of the Camino trace back to medieval times when pilgrims traveled to the cathedral in Santiago de Compostela in northern Spain, believed to house the remains of St. James. For many, this was a pilgrimage of penance, healing, or simply seeking meaning in their lives. Over the centuries, the Camino has evolved into a path walked by people from all backgrounds and beliefs, each bringing their own reasons for embarking on this timeless journey.

This journey through Spanish landscapes, towns, and countryside is steeped in history, and each step is a part of a larger, centuries-old tradition.

Types of Camino Routes: Which Path to Choose?

There's more than one way to Santiago, each path with its own scenery, challenges, and highlights. Choosing a route is one of the most exciting parts of planning, as each path offers a unique experience:

Camino Francés (The French Way): The most popular and well-traveled route, starting from Saint-Jean-Pied-de-Port in France. This route covers over 780 kilometers and offers everything from mountainous views to medieval villages, making it the classic Camino choice for many first-timers.

Camino Portugués (The Portuguese Way): Starting in Lisbon or Porto, this route is known for its coastal views and mild terrain. The Camino Portugués appeals to those looking for a quieter path with scenic coastal sections and quaint villages.

Camino del Norte (The Northern Way): Following the northern coast of Spain, this route provides breathtaking views of the Bay of Biscay. It's known for its rugged terrain and is ideal for those seeking a more challenging hike.

Camino Primitivo (The Original Way): Believed to be the oldest route, this trail is both shorter and more physically demanding. Starting in Oviedo, it leads through mountainous areas and is a favorite for pilgrims seeking solitude and a deeper connection with nature.

Each of these routes offers a blend of landscapes, from bustling cities to quiet rural towns, coastal scenes to forest trails. Choosing a route depends on your level of fitness, time availability, and the type of experience you're after. Whether you go for the well-traveled Camino Francés or the solitary Camino Primitivo, every path to Santiago holds its own treasures.

Benefits of Walking the Camino

While the Camino has deep spiritual roots, modern pilgrims walk for many reasons beyond faith. Some seek a break from their busy lives, hoping to reconnect with themselves in a simpler, slower way of life. Others enjoy the physical challenge and the camaraderie among travelers from around the world. Walking the Camino provides numerous benefits:

Physical Health: Covering miles daily builds endurance, strength, and overall fitness. Walking the Camino can be challenging, but the physical effort and endurance it requires make it a rewarding way to improve health.

Mental Clarity: The Camino's rhythm of walking, resting, and being in nature can bring a sense of calm and mental clarity. Many pilgrims find that the Camino helps them reflect on their lives and gain new perspectives.

Spiritual Fulfillment: For those drawn to the Camino's spiritual side, the experience can deepen faith, offer healing, or provide a time for prayer and reflection. The Camino is a space where many feel a special connection to a purpose larger than themselves.

Social Connections: Walking the Camino often involves meeting people from around the world. Pilgrims share stories, help each other through challenges, and form connections that can last a lifetime.

Whether it's improving your fitness, seeking mental clarity, or looking for a meaningful travel experience, the Camino provides all this and more. The journey is as transformative as it is physical, and every pilgrim comes away with something new.

Preparing Your Mind and Body for the Journey

Preparation is key to enjoying and completing the Camino. The journey isn't just a physical endeavor; it's an emotional and mental commitment. Preparing yourself physically by walking regularly, breaking in your shoes, and getting accustomed to carrying a backpack is crucial for a successful Camino experience.

But equally important is preparing your mind. Walking for days or even weeks takes patience, resilience, and an openness to the unknown. Challenges like unpredictable weather, physical fatigue, and even loneliness are all part of the Camino experience.

Many pilgrims find it helpful to set intentions for their journey, whether they're walking in memory of a loved one, seeking clarity in life, or embracing a new adventure.

This introduction provides a foundation for anyone beginning their journey on the Camino de Santiago. From understanding its history to choosing the best route and preparing physically and mentally, this book is here to guide you. The Camino is a path rich with stories, experiences, and connections, and as you read through these pages, you'll find all the tools you need to make the most of this once-in-a-lifetime adventure.

Chapter 1: Getting Started: Planning Your Camino

Planning a Camino de Santiago pilgrimage is both exciting and a little overwhelming. There are many routes to choose from, each with its own highlights, challenges, and unique flavor. Knowing when to go, which route to take, how long it might take, and what kind of budget to set can make a big difference in how enjoyable and fulfilling your journey becomes. This chapter breaks down the essentials of planning, guiding you through the key decisions that will shape your Camino experience.

When to Walk: Best Seasons and Weather Conditions

The Camino can be walked year-round, but choosing the best season depends on your personal preferences, physical resilience, and tolerance for crowds. Each season on the Camino comes with its own weather conditions, advantages, and challenges.

Spring (March to May): Spring is a popular time to walk, with moderate temperatures and vibrant landscapes full of blooming flowers and green fields. Days are comfortably cool, especially in April and May. However, spring can be rainy, so come prepared with waterproof clothing and gear. While March is quieter, by May, the Camino is bustling with fellow pilgrims.

Summer (June to August): Summer is the most popular season due to warm weather, long days, and vacation periods in Europe. However, it also means larger crowds, especially on the Camino Francés, with many albergues (hostels) filling up quickly. Temperatures in some areas, especially the Meseta (Spain's central plateau), can reach high levels, making hydration and sun protection essential. For those seeking solitude, this may not be the ideal season, but the energy and camaraderie are unmistakable.

Fall (September to November): Fall is another favorite season among pilgrims, particularly in September and October when the crowds lessen, and temperatures are cooler. September still enjoys long days and warm weather, making it ideal for those who want a peaceful experience without extreme conditions. By late October and November, temperatures drop, rain increases, and some albergues may close for the season. Still, the changing autumn leaves make the landscapes along the Camino especially beautiful.

Winter (December to February): Winter is the quietest and coldest season on the Camino, but it can be a rewarding time for pilgrims seeking solitude. The routes are less crowded, and accommodation is generally easier to find, though many albergues close. Winter on the Camino del Norte and in mountainous areas can be harsh, with snow and icy trails. For those considering a winter Camino, the Camino Portugués and southern sections of the Camino Francés offer milder conditions.

Choosing the Right Camino Route for You

There are multiple routes leading to Santiago de Compostela, each with unique terrain, scenery, and challenges. Here's a look at some of the most popular routes to help you decide which one might best suit your needs and interests.

Camino Francés: The Classic Route

The Camino Francés (French Way) is the most well-known and widely walked route, stretching approximately 780 kilometers (485 miles) from Saint-Jean-Pied-de-Port in France to

Santiago de Compostela. It's the route with the most infrastructure, featuring numerous albergues, restaurants, and support services along the way.

Highlights: This route offers a diverse mix of landscapes, from the Pyrenees mountains to vineyards, farmlands, and medieval towns. Key stops along the way include Pamplona, known for its annual running of the bulls; Burgos, with its stunning Gothic cathedral; and León, another city with rich historical sites.

Challenges: The Camino Francés can be physically demanding, especially the initial ascent over the Pyrenees. Additionally, it's the most popular route, so expect large crowds, particularly in summer.

Who It's Best For: The Camino Francés is ideal for first-time pilgrims or those seeking a traditional Camino experience with plenty of amenities and a strong sense of community.

Camino Portugués: A Coastal Alternative

The Camino Portugués (Portuguese Way) begins in Lisbon or Porto and travels through Portugal into Spain, covering around 610 kilometers (380 miles) from Lisbon or 260 kilometers (160 miles) from Porto. It offers both an inland and a coastal route, with the coastal path being particularly scenic.

Highlights: From Lisbon, you'll pass historic sites, rolling hills, and eucalyptus forests. The coastal route from Porto provides beautiful ocean views and beach towns, making it a refreshing alternative to inland routes. Santiago-bound, you'll experience Portuguese hospitality, excellent seafood, and a mix of urban and rural settings.

Challenges: While less physically demanding than the Camino Francés, the Camino Portugués has sections with long distances between albergues. The coastal route can be windy, especially in the northern part.

Who It's Best For: This route suits those looking for a quieter experience, with a mix of ocean views and historical cities. It's ideal for pilgrims seeking a scenic alternative to the more crowded routes.

Camino del Norte: The Scenic Northern Path

The Camino del Norte (Northern Way) runs along the northern coast of Spain, following the Bay of Biscay for approximately 825 kilometers (512 miles) from Irún near the French border to Santiago. It's known for its rugged beauty and dramatic coastal landscapes.

Highlights: The route offers stunning coastal scenery, including beaches, cliffs, and fishing villages, as well as the chance to explore Basque culture and cuisine. Major cities along the way include Bilbao, home to the Guggenheim Museum, and San Sebastián, famous for its culinary scene.

Challenges: The Camino del Norte is one of the more challenging routes due to its hilly terrain and frequent elevation changes. Weather along the coast can be unpredictable, and the route has fewer albergues than the Camino Francés, requiring some planning.

Who It's Best For: This route is suited to experienced hikers or those seeking a quieter, more physically challenging Camino. The Northern Way is less crowded and offers a chance to experience Spain's scenic coast.

Camino Primitivo: The Original Path

The Camino Primitivo (Original Way) is the oldest Camino route, believed to be the original path taken by early pilgrims. It starts in Oviedo and runs about 320 kilometers (200 miles) to Santiago. This route is known for its mountainous terrain and tranquil landscapes.

Highlights: The Camino Primitivo offers a true back-to-nature experience with lush green mountains, forests, and peaceful rural areas. Highlights include the stunning Asturian landscape, small villages, and a deep sense of Camino history.

Challenges: The Primitivo is one of the most physically demanding routes, with steep ascents and descents. It requires good fitness and hiking experience, as the terrain can be rugged, especially in wet weather.

Who It's Best For: This route is ideal for experienced hikers or those seeking a remote, less-traveled Camino. The Camino Primitivo offers solitude and a challenging trek for pilgrims ready for a more adventurous journey.

How Many Days to Walk Each Route?

The duration of your Camino depends on your chosen route, daily distance, and pace. Here's a rough guide for the average time it takes to complete each route:

Camino Francés: 30-35 days, assuming an average of 20-25 kilometers per day.

Camino Portugués: 25-30 days from Lisbon, or around 10-14 days from Porto.

Camino del Norte: 35-40 days, covering 20-25 kilometers per day on hilly terrain.

Camino Primitivo: 12-15 days, as it's a shorter route but with more challenging terrain.

Most pilgrims aim for around 20-25 kilometers (12-15 miles) per day, with occasional rest days in larger cities or areas of interest. Planning rest days helps prevent fatigue and gives you time to explore cultural sites and historic towns along the way.

Setting a Budget: Daily Costs and Saving Tips

Budgeting for the Camino is essential, as daily costs can add up, especially on longer routes. Here's a breakdown of what you can expect and some tips for keeping costs manageable.

Accommodation: Basic albergues typically cost €5-15 per night, while private hostels or hotels range from €20-60, depending on the location and amenities. Planning to stay in albergues most nights can significantly reduce costs.

Food: Many towns along the Camino offer a "Menu del Peregrino" (Pilgrim's Menu), a three-course meal that costs around €10-15. Groceries and snacks can be inexpensive, and some albergues have kitchens for self-catering. Plan to spend around €20-30 per day on food.

Transportation: If you plan to take a bus or train to your starting point or back to the airport, factor in transportation costs. Most routes are accessible by public transportation, with costs varying depending on distance.

Miscellaneous: Don't forget expenses for laundry, personal items, and occasional indulgences like a café stop or a souvenir. Budget around €5-10 per day for these extras.

Sample Budget for the Camino Francés:

Accommodation: €10-15 per night x 30 days = €300-450

Food: €20 per day x 30 days = €600

Miscellaneous: €5 per day x 30 days = €150

Total: Approximately €1,050-1,200 for a 30-day journey on the Camino

Francés. To save money, consider packing your own meals, avoiding peak tourist seasons, and choosing budget accommodations.

Budgeting wisely and staying flexible allows you to enjoy your Camino experience without financial stress. The Camino offers options for every budget, and with careful planning, you can make the most of your resources while enjoying the journey.

Chapter 2: Packing Essentials for the Camino de Santiago

Preparing for the Camino de Santiago involves making smart choices about what you'll carry with you every step of the way. The right gear and packing strategy can make a significant difference in your comfort, endurance, and overall experience. This chapter covers everything from essential items and clothing to tips on selecting the best backpack and footwear, along with advice on travel-friendly gadgets that can enhance your journey.

Packing List: Gear, Clothing, and Essentials

Packing for the Camino requires a balanced approach; you want to be prepared without overloading yourself. Here's a breakdown of the essentials you'll need:

Clothing Essentials: Stick to lightweight, moisture-wicking, and quick-drying clothing. Consider packing:

T-shirts (2-3) in a breathable fabric like merino wool or polyester
Long-sleeved shirt for cooler mornings or protection from the sun
Lightweight fleece or down jacket for warmth in the early mornings or evenings
Convertible pants or hiking shorts (1-2 pairs) that offer flexibility
Underwear and socks: Quick-dry, moisture-wicking options are best. Blister-resistant socks are highly recommended.
Sleepwear and comfortable change of clothes for evenings
Waterproof rain jacket or poncho: The weather can change quickly, and staying dry is essential.
Personal Items:
Toiletries: Toothbrush, toothpaste, small bar of soap, microfiber towel, and travel-sized shampoo
First-aid kit: Blister prevention (such as blister pads or moleskin), bandages, ibuprofen, antiseptic wipes, and any personal medications
Sun protection: Sunscreen, hat, sunglasses, and lip balm with SPF
Multi-tool or Swiss Army knife: Useful for food prep, repairs, and general needs
Sleeping Essentials:
Sleeping bag or lightweight sleep sack: Albergues (hostels) often have bedding, but a sleep sack can be helpful for extra warmth or cleanliness.

Earplugs and eye mask: Albergues can be noisy with other pilgrims, and these can help ensure a restful night.

Other Essentials:

Water bottle or hydration system: Staying hydrated is crucial, and a reusable bottle saves money and reduces waste.

Lightweight, collapsible hiking poles: Many find that these reduce strain, especially on the knees, during steep climbs or descents.

Guidebook and/or Camino map: Handy for navigation and information on upcoming stops.

Choosing the Right Backpack

Your backpack will become one of the most important pieces of gear, as it will carry everything you need throughout the journey. Aim to choose a pack that's comfortable, durable, and the right size for your needs.

Size and Capacity: Look for a backpack with a capacity of 30-40 liters. Anything smaller might be too tight, while larger packs can tempt you to overpack. This size should be sufficient for carrying essentials without overburdening you.

Fit and Comfort: Backpacks come in various sizes, so consider your torso length and body size when choosing one. Many backpacks are adjustable to fit comfortably on your shoulders and hips. The weight should sit on your hips, not your shoulders, so look for padded hip belts and shoulder straps.

Ventilation and Support: Look for a pack with a breathable back panel, which can keep your back from overheating. Internal frames provide structure and keep the load balanced, which is ideal for longer hikes like the Camino.

Additional Features:

Rain cover: While you can buy this separately, many packs include a rain cover to protect your gear.

Pockets and compartments: Easily accessible pockets for water bottles, snacks, and frequently used items are helpful.

Compression straps: These help stabilize the load and make the pack feel more compact.

Footwear: Finding Comfortable and Durable Hiking Boots

Comfortable, durable footwear is essential for the Camino de Santiago, as you'll be walking long distances on a variety of terrains. Choosing the right pair of hiking boots or shoes can make or break your experience.

Hiking Boots vs. Trail Shoes: Decide whether you prefer the stability of hiking boots or the lighter feel of trail shoes. Boots provide more ankle support and are better suited for rugged terrain, while trail shoes are lighter and often more breathable. Whichever you choose, make sure they're broken in before you start.

Fit: Your shoes should be snug enough to prevent your feet from sliding around, but they shouldn't pinch or cause discomfort. Leave a little extra room in the toe box to prevent blisters, as feet can swell over long distances.

Waterproofing: Many hikers opt for waterproof shoes to protect against rain and morning dew, but some prefer more breathable, non-waterproof options, especially if walking in warmer months. Waterproof shoes can feel warmer but will keep your feet dry in wet conditions.

Socks and Blister Prevention: Blister-resistant socks, like those made from merino wool or synthetic blends, help reduce moisture and friction. Bring a few pairs and rotate them daily. Some hikers also use sock liners for added blister protection.

Travel Light: Packing Tips to Minimize Weight

Packing light is essential on the Camino, as a heavy load can quickly lead to fatigue and strain. Aim to carry no more than 10% of your body weight, ideally staying under 8 kilograms (about 17 pounds). Here are some ways to keep your pack light:

Pack Multi-Purpose Items: Choose versatile clothing that can be layered or worn multiple ways. Convertible pants, for example, can serve as both pants and shorts.

Minimize Toiletries and First-Aid Supplies: Take travel-sized toiletries, and consider buying refills along the way rather than overpacking.

Cut Down on Clothing: You'll have chances to wash clothes in albergues, so bring just a few changes. Two or three tops and bottoms, along with essentials like underwear and socks, should suffice.

Use Compression Bags: These help reduce bulk by compressing clothes and other soft items.

Opt for Lightweight Gear: Invest in lightweight, compact gear, including a light sleeping bag, microfiber towel, and collapsible hiking poles.

Gadgets and Accessories: Navigating with Technology

While the Camino can be a time to disconnect, a few gadgets and accessories can enhance your experience and help you stay organized. Here are a few tech essentials:

Smartphone: Useful for navigation apps, staying connected with loved ones, and capturing memories. Download offline maps, such as Google Maps or a dedicated Camino app, so you can find your way without relying on a signal.

Power Bank: Many pilgrims find themselves running out of battery on the trail, so a power bank can keep your devices charged. Look for a compact, lightweight option that provides multiple charges.

Camera: If you want high-quality photos, consider bringing a small digital camera. Many pilgrims are satisfied with their smartphone cameras, but some prefer a dedicated camera for capturing the Camino's beauty.

Headlamp or Small Flashlight: This is handy for early morning starts, especially if you don't want to disturb others by turning on lights in albergues.

E-Reader or Small Journal: For downtime, an e-reader is lighter than carrying books. Many pilgrims also bring a journal to record thoughts and experiences along the way.

Lightweight Locks: Small, combination locks can keep your belongings secure when staying in shared accommodations.

Packing for the Camino de Santiago requires careful planning, but with the right choices, you'll be well-prepared for a rewarding experience. By focusing on essentials, choosing quality gear, and keeping your pack light, you'll be able to walk comfortably and make the most of every step on the Camino.

Chapter 3: Navigating the Camino: Maps, Signs, and Apps

Getting around on the Camino de Santiago is often a simple pleasure, as the routes are generally well-marked, and signs are there to guide you through towns, fields, forests, and everything in between. That said, having some basic tools and knowledge in place can make your experience even smoother and more enjoyable. This chapter covers the essentials: understanding the Camino's waymarks and signs, using helpful apps and GPS, navigating remote areas, and staying safe along the way.

Reading Camino Waymarks and Signs

One of the best aspects of the Camino is how straightforward it is to follow. You'll find distinctive waymarks along each route, which have been placed specifically to help guide you toward Santiago. The most common symbols are:

The Yellow Arrow: By far the most recognized waymark, this bright yellow arrow points you in the direction of Santiago. You'll find it painted on trees, buildings, rocks, fences, and even the ground. Keep your eyes peeled for these arrows, as they're often placed in areas where the path isn't obvious.

The Scallop Shell: Another iconic Camino symbol, the scallop shell, serves as a guide. Often displayed on posts, signs, or plaques, the shell's "rays" generally indicate the direction toward Santiago. On official markers, such as milestones, the narrow end of the shell points toward Santiago.

Stone Markers: In some regions, especially in Galicia, you'll find stone markers with engraved scallop shells and arrows. These markers also often display the remaining distance to Santiago, giving you a boost of encouragement as you near your destination.

City and Village Signs: Passing through towns and villages, you'll encounter street signs and symbols that confirm you're on the right path. These might also point out landmarks, albergues (hostels), or directions to food stops.

Learning to trust these waymarks and symbols will save you from unnecessary detours. If you're ever uncertain, you can also look for other pilgrims—someone is usually close by, and a quick question can get you back on track.

Using Apps and GPS for Navigation

While traditional waymarks are reliable, having digital tools on hand can provide an extra layer of confidence. In recent years, apps and GPS have become helpful companions for modern pilgrims. Here are some popular apps that many find useful:

Camino Pilgrim (Wise Pilgrim Guides): This app covers most routes with maps, profiles, and a listing of accommodations and services. You can use it offline, which is a plus if you're in an area with limited connectivity.

Buen Camino: This app has helpful features, such as route maps, directions, and details about nearby accommodations and landmarks. It also includes a social component, allowing you to connect with other pilgrims nearby.

Google Maps: Though not specific to the Camino, Google Maps can still be helpful, especially for finding specific places like hostels, restaurants, or landmarks. You can download maps of certain areas for offline use if you know you'll be without service.

Maps.me: A GPS app with detailed offline maps, Maps.me allows you to download specific regions, which can be helpful for rural or remote areas. It's a good backup for tracking your route if you're off the main path.

While these apps are useful, remember that relying solely on them can detract from the experience of following the traditional signs and waymarks. Use them as a backup or for additional information, but try to keep your primary focus on the physical markers that have guided pilgrims for generations.

Finding Your Way in Remote Areas

Most of the Camino routes pass through small towns, villages, and rural landscapes where the paths are well-marked. However, there are sections, especially in more isolated regions, where you may not see a waymark for a while. Here's how to handle these stretches:

Stay Alert to Subtle Signs: In remote areas, waymarks might be less obvious—small arrows on rocks or faded paint marks. Keep an eye out, especially around junctions or trail intersections.

Follow the Beaten Path: Even if waymarks are sparse, the Camino trails are usually well-trodden. If you find yourself on an overgrown or unused trail, double-check your route and look for signs you may have missed.

Use Your Apps Wisely: In places where you feel uncertain, consult an app to confirm your direction. You can open a downloaded map or check your GPS location to ensure you're still headed toward the next town.

Ask Locals for Help: In remote areas, locals are often familiar with the Camino routes and can point you in the right direction. A friendly "¿Por dónde está el Camino?" (Where is the Camino?) can go a long way in getting you back on track.

Sometimes, these remote areas offer some of the most serene, beautiful moments on the Camino. With a few navigation basics, you can confidently handle these stretches and make the most of them.

Tips for Staying Safe on the Trail

Safety is generally not a major concern on the Camino, as it's a well-traveled route, and the community atmosphere means that fellow pilgrims and locals are often willing to help. However, there are a few tips to keep in mind to ensure a smooth journey:

Stay Hydrated and Take Breaks: Walking for hours, especially under the sun, can be tiring. Always carry enough water and take regular breaks to avoid exhaustion.

Carry a Basic First Aid Kit: Blisters are one of the most common issues for pilgrims. Pack essentials like bandages, blister pads, and antiseptic wipes. A small first aid kit can help with minor injuries or discomforts along the way.

Keep Valuables Secure: While theft is rare, it's wise to keep your valuables close. Use a money belt or secure pocket for essentials like your passport, cash, and credit cards.

Be Aware of Weather Conditions: The weather on the Camino can change quickly, especially in mountainous or coastal areas. Check the forecast and pack appropriately for rain, heat, or cold. A lightweight rain poncho or waterproof jacket is worth the space in your pack.

Don't Walk Alone at Night: While many parts of the Camino are safe even in the early morning or evening, it's better to avoid walking alone in the dark. Stick with a group or wait for daylight to continue.

Listen to Your Body: It's easy to push yourself on the Camino, but rest when you need to. Overexertion can lead to injuries, and taking it slow will help you reach Santiago in good health.

Know Emergency Numbers: Save emergency contacts and the local number for ambulance services (112 in Spain) on your phone, just in case.

While the Camino community is very supportive, it's wise to be prepared.

By understanding the waymarks, using technology wisely, being prepared for remote areas, and staying safe on the trail, you can fully enjoy the freedom and adventure that comes with walking the Camino. As you travel through villages, forests, and fields, keep your mind on the journey ahead and enjoy each day as it unfolds. The path will guide you, and with these tools in hand, you'll be able to focus on making lasting memories on your way to Santiago.

Chapter 4: Accommodation on the Camino

Finding the right place to rest each night is one of the most important parts of your Camino experience. With options ranging from basic, pilgrim-friendly albergues to hotels with private amenities, the Camino offers a range of accommodations that fit different needs, budgets, and preferences. This chapter breaks down the types of places you'll find along the way, highlights some of the best albergues, and offers practical tips to help you book and make the most of your stay.

Types of Accommodation: Hostels, Albergues, and Hotels

Albergues (Pilgrim Hostels): The most popular and affordable option for pilgrims, albergues offer a basic but comfortable stay. They're usually large dormitory-style rooms with bunk beds and shared facilities, designed to foster a community spirit. Albergues come in various types:

Municipal Albergues: Run by local governments, these are typically low-cost, sometimes charging only a few euros. They can't be booked in advance and operate on a first-come, first-served basis. While they offer only the basics, they are often located in central spots and provide a genuine pilgrim experience.

Private Albergues: Privately owned and sometimes offering extras like Wi-Fi, kitchens, and laundry facilities. These are slightly more expensive than municipal options but provide more comfort and flexibility, often allowing for advance bookings.

Parochial or Donativo Albergues: Run by churches or local communities and funded through donations ("donativo"). These albergues focus on the spiritual and community aspects of the Camino. Meals are often provided communally, and donations are encouraged but not required. Staying in a donativo albergue can be a unique and humbling experience.

Hostels: For pilgrims seeking a little more privacy, hostels are a middle-ground option. They're more expensive than albergues but generally have private or semi-private rooms.

Hostels often offer better amenities, like private bathrooms and smaller shared spaces, and may have communal kitchens or cafés. Some hostels are explicitly pilgrim-friendly, offering special rates or amenities for those on the Camino.

Hotels and Casas Rurales: If you want complete privacy and comfort after a long day's walk, hotels and casas rurales (rural guesthouses) are ideal. Though they come at a higher price, they offer private rooms, bathrooms, and sometimes in-house dining options. Hotels along the Camino range from basic to luxury, and casas rurales often have a charming, local feel, providing a chance to experience the region's hospitality more intimately.

Top-Rated Albergues to Stay In

Finding a great albergue can add a memorable touch to your Camino journey. Here are some highly recommended albergues that pilgrims frequently praise for their warmth, hospitality, and welcoming atmosphere:

Albergue de Roncesvalles (Camino Francés): Located in the historic town of Roncesvalles, this albergue is well-known for its spacious dorms and beautiful surroundings. It's a great starting point for many pilgrims and offers an ideal place to rest after a challenging first day.

Albergue de San Nicolás (near Itero de la Vega, Camino Francés): Run by the Italian Confraternity of St. James, this unique albergue operates on a donation basis and offers pilgrims a simple but warm welcome, often involving a traditional foot-washing ceremony. It's a favorite for those seeking a spiritual experience.

Albergue Güemes (Camino del Norte): Located on the Camino del Norte, this albergue is known for its friendly host, Ernesto, who shares stories and insights about the Camino. It offers pilgrims a welcoming, communal experience with meals provided.

Albergue Casa Susi (near Grañón, Camino Francés): This charming albergue is run by hosts who genuinely care about creating a warm and comfortable environment. Meals are shared communally, making it a popular spot for pilgrims looking to connect with others.

Albergue de la Piedra (near Villafranca del Bierzo, Camino Francés): Set in a beautiful location, this albergue has a cozy atmosphere with an outdoor terrace. It offers great food, friendly service, and a restful environment.

Staying in these top-rated albergues can add a touch of comfort and community to your Camino experience. Each offers a special memory, a chance to meet fellow pilgrims, and a unique perspective on the Camino spirit.

Booking Tips and Reservations

Municipal and Parochial Albergues: These don't typically allow reservations, so they work on a first-come, first-served basis. Arrive earlier in the afternoon, especially in busy months, to secure a spot.

Private Albergues and Hostels: Most private albergues and hostels offer online booking. Apps like Camino Ninja and Wise Pilgrim can help you find and book these options, especially in busy towns.

Hotels and Casas Rurales: Booking ahead is recommended if you prefer private rooms, particularly in peak seasons. Major towns along the route have hotel listings on sites like Booking.com, or you can book directly on the hotel's website.

Flexibility: If you're unsure of your daily mileage, it's wise to mix booked accommodations with open-ended days. This gives you flexibility while ensuring a spot on certain nights, especially at popular stops.

Cancellations: Check cancellation policies before booking. This can be useful if you need to adjust your plans or take a rest day.

Budget-Friendly Lodging Options

Walking the Camino can be affordable, especially with the right choices. Here are some ways to keep lodging costs down:

Stick with Municipal Albergues: These are the cheapest accommodation options, often costing between €5-10 per night. While basic, they provide a clean, safe place to sleep and the opportunity to connect with other pilgrims.

Donativo Albergues: Though donations are encouraged, these places rely on the kindness of pilgrims to sustain them. Donativo albergues can make your Camino affordable while giving back to the Camino community.

Mix in Private Albergues Sparingly: If you need a night with better amenities, choose private albergues, which generally cost €10-15 per night. Many provide added comforts like Wi-Fi, kitchens, and laundry facilities, so they're a good choice for rest days.

Skip Hotels Except for Treat Nights: Hotels are the most expensive option. Consider staying in one occasionally as a treat or if you need extra privacy, but relying on them regularly can add significantly to your budget.

Budget-friendly accommodations allow you to stretch your money further and connect more closely with other pilgrims. Many find that the simplest stays are the most rewarding.

Sleeping Tips for Shared Spaces

Staying in shared spaces is part of the Camino experience and can be enjoyable with a few tips to help make it comfortable:

Earplugs and Eye Mask: These are essential. Earplugs help with snoring or other night noises, while an eye mask can block out early morning light.

Quiet Packing: Pack your bag the night before, especially if you plan to leave early. Using a flashlight instead of the main light helps you respect other pilgrims' sleep.

Stick to Your Bed: Space is limited, so try to keep your items on or around your bed. This keeps common areas clear and helps everyone stay organized.

Respect Quiet Hours: Most albergues have quiet hours from 10 p.m. to 6 a.m. Avoid talking or making noise during these times, especially in dormitory rooms.

Be Courteous: A little kindness goes a long way. A smile, helping hand, or respecting shared space makes the stay enjoyable for everyone.

Sleeping in shared spaces can be a new experience, but with these tips, it can also be a great opportunity to connect with other pilgrims while ensuring a good rest.

With this guide to Camino accommodation, you'll be ready to find the right place to rest each night, make the most of the albergues, and connect with fellow pilgrims along the way. The Camino is about more than the walk; it's about sharing space, stories, and a common journey. This chapter ensures you're prepared to find affordable, comfortable, and welcoming places to stay every step of the way.

Chapter 5: Camino Diet: Eating Well on the Trail

Eating well on the Camino de Santiago is essential to keep your energy up and make your experience enjoyable. As you walk through various Spanish regions, you'll encounter an array of traditional foods, unique flavors, and meals tailored for pilgrims. This chapter will guide you on what to eat, where to find budget-friendly meals, and how to cater to special dietary needs.

Traditional Spanish Cuisine to Try

One of the pleasures of walking the Camino is experiencing Spain's rich culinary culture. Each region along the Camino has its specialties, so here are some must-try dishes:

Pulpo a la Gallega (Galician Octopus): In Galicia, octopus is a popular dish, prepared with a sprinkle of paprika and olive oil. You'll find it in markets and restaurants, especially in towns like Melide, where this dish is a local favorite.

Tortilla Española (Spanish Omelet): A thick omelet made with potatoes and onions, often served as a tapa or filling breakfast. You'll find this staple in most towns, either served warm or at room temperature. It's filling, affordable, and easy to carry for later.

Pimientos de Padrón (Padrón Peppers): These small green peppers are grilled and sprinkled with coarse salt. Be prepared – while most are mild, some can be quite spicy! They're often found as a shared dish in northern Spain.

Chorizo and Jamón: Spanish cured meats, especially the famous jamón ibérico and chorizo, are commonly served in albergues and bars. Try them in sandwiches, on their own, or as part of a pilgrim menu.

Caldo Gallego (Galician Soup): A hearty, warm soup made with greens, potatoes, and sometimes beans or ham. Perfect for chilly days, this soup is especially common in Galicia.

Empanada Gallega: This Galician pie, filled with tuna, meat, or vegetables, is a popular choice for pilgrims, as it's easy to carry and enjoy on the go. Look for it at bakeries and cafes along the way.

Where to Find the Best Pilgrim Menus

Most towns along the Camino offer a "menú del peregrino" or pilgrim menu, which provides a set three-course meal for a reasonable price. These menus cater specifically to pilgrims, offering filling, balanced meals that won't break the bank. Here are a few tips on finding great pilgrim menus:

Typical Menu Options: Most pilgrim menus include a starter (like soup, salad, or pasta), a main course (such as grilled meat or fish), and dessert. Wine and bread are usually included. Portions are generous, making this a great option after a long day of walking.

Where to Look: Many albergues, bars, and restaurants along the Camino offer pilgrim menus, especially in popular towns like Pamplona, Burgos, and León. You'll often see signs outside advertising the menu, so keep an eye out as you walk into town.

Best Times to Eat: Dinner service usually starts around 7:00 p.m., though some places may open earlier for pilgrims. Lunch is typically between 1:00 p.m. and 3:00 p.m. Eating at these times ensures you get a fresh, warm meal.

Regional Favorites: In Navarra and La Rioja, expect hearty stews and plenty of red wine. As you enter Galicia, you'll find more seafood dishes, with an emphasis on local fish and octopus. Don't hesitate to ask locals or fellow pilgrims for their recommendations.

Budget Tips for Food and Drink

Walking the Camino can be affordable if you know how to manage your food expenses. Here are some budget-friendly strategies for eating well without overspending:

Shop at Local Markets: Most towns have markets where you can buy fresh bread, cheese, fruit, and snacks. Stocking up on these essentials can help you avoid pricier restaurant meals for lunch.

Choose Albergue Meals: Many albergues offer communal meals for a small fee. These meals are often homemade, generous, and a great way to meet fellow pilgrims. Some albergues also have kitchen facilities where you can prepare your own food.

Order Tapas Instead of Full Meals: In Spain, ordering a few tapas (small dishes) can be an affordable way to sample a variety of foods. Try ordering several tapas to share with other pilgrims for a lighter, social meal.

Drink Tap Water: Tap water is generally safe to drink along the Camino, so bring a refillable bottle. Buying bottled water can add up over time, so refilling your bottle at fountains and taps in towns helps keep costs down.

Look for Menú del Día: Outside of the pilgrim menu, many restaurants offer a "menú del día" (menu of the day) at lunchtime, which is similar in price and structure to the pilgrim menu. It's a filling meal option if you're passing through a town during the day.

Healthy Snacks for Energy and Stamina

Snacking on the trail is important to maintain energy between meals. Here are some portable, healthy snacks that are easy to find and pack:

Nuts and Seeds: High in protein and healthy fats, nuts like almonds, walnuts, and sunflower seeds make for convenient, energizing snacks.

Fruit: Fresh fruit like apples, bananas, and oranges are widely available and easy to carry. Dried fruit like raisins or apricots are lightweight and have a longer shelf life.

Cheese and Bread: Spanish bread and cheese are filling and provide the carbs and protein you need to keep walking. Many grocery stores sell small portions of cheese, which are easy to pack and enjoy on the go.

Energy Bars: You can find energy bars at supermarkets and pharmacies, or bring some from home if you have a preferred brand. They're compact, lightweight, and provide a quick boost.

Dark Chocolate: For a little treat, dark chocolate is both tasty and energizing. It's less likely to melt in warm weather and is a good source of quick energy.

Dietary Considerations: Vegetarian, Vegan, and Gluten-Free Options

Finding vegetarian, vegan, and gluten-free food on the Camino is possible, though it may require some planning. Here's how to manage dietary needs:

Vegetarian Options: The pilgrim menu usually offers vegetarian-friendly starters like salads, vegetable soups, and tortilla española. For mains, you may find pasta or rice dishes, though protein options can be limited. Consider supplementing with nuts or cheese from local stores.

Vegan Options: Vegans may find it more challenging, especially in rural areas. Stick to salads, bread with olive oil, and dishes like patatas bravas (fried potatoes) when eating out. Stock up on fruits, vegetables, and nuts when possible, and seek out larger supermarkets in cities for vegan options.

Gluten-Free Options: While bread is a staple of the Spanish diet, gluten-free alternatives are available in larger supermarkets. Look for naturally gluten-free foods like rice, potatoes, meat, cheese, and fruits. If you're very sensitive, bring some gluten-free snacks from home, as cross-contamination can be an issue in smaller kitchens.

Learn Key Phrases: Learning a few key phrases in Spanish can make a big difference. Phrases like "Soy vegetariano/a" (I'm vegetarian), "No como carne" (I don't eat meat), and "Sin gluten, por favor" (Gluten-free, please) will help you communicate your needs more easily.

Eating well on the Camino de Santiago doesn't have to be complicated or expensive. With a little planning, you can enjoy a range of delicious Spanish dishes, find meals that fit your budget, and meet your dietary needs. Whether you're savoring local specialties, sharing a meal with fellow pilgrims, or enjoying a snack by the trail, food on the Camino is part of the experience, giving you the energy and connection needed to reach Santiago.

Chapter 6: Hidden Gems Along the Camino de Santiago

The Camino de Santiago isn't just about reaching Santiago; it's also about discovering the countless hidden gems that make the journey memorable. From secluded villages and breathtaking viewpoints to local festivals and nature escapes, these off-the-beaten-path stops give the Camino its charm and personality. This chapter brings you some of the Camino's best-kept secrets—places you won't want to miss.

Must-See Villages and Towns Off the Beaten Path

One of the best parts of the Camino is the chance to explore lesser-known villages and towns. These places offer a glimpse of Spanish culture and tradition and are often filled with welcoming locals eager to share their stories and customs.

O Cebreiro (Camino Francés): Perched in the mountains of Galicia, O Cebreiro is famous for its ancient stone houses known as "pallozas" and its stunning church, Santa María la Real. The views over the surrounding valleys are breathtaking, especially at sunrise or sunset. The village is small, but its charm and history make it a must-visit on the Camino.

Castrojeriz (Camino Francés): This town is a journey through history with its Romanesque churches and the ruins of a hilltop castle. Castrojeriz is also known for its wide-open landscapes and quiet streets, providing a peaceful break for pilgrims. Take time to visit the Gothic Church of Nuestra Señora del Manzano and enjoy the village's relaxed pace.

Muxía (Camino Finisterre): If you're continuing to the Atlantic after Santiago, Muxía is a treasure at the end of the road. Known for its wild coastline, stunning beaches, and the mystical Sanctuary of A Virxe da Barca, Muxía offers a truly Galician experience. Local legend holds that St. James was visited here by the Virgin Mary, adding to its spiritual importance.

Santillana del Mar (Camino del Norte): Known as "the town of three lies" (it's neither a saintly town, flat, nor by the sea), Santillana del Mar is filled with cobbled streets, medieval architecture, and a romantic atmosphere. It's home to the Collegiate Church of Santa Juliana and is famous for the Altamira Caves, known as the "Sistine Chapel of Prehistoric Art."

Scenic Detours and Viewpoints

While the main route has plenty to offer, a few detours and viewpoints are worth the extra steps for the scenery and sense of discovery.

Alto del Perdón (Camino Francés): Just outside Pamplona, this iconic hill offers sweeping views of the surrounding countryside. The iron sculptures of pilgrims at the top make for a great photo spot and a chance to pause and take in the panoramic views. It's a bit of a climb, but the experience is worth every step.

Montes de Oca (Camino Francés): Known as the "Mountains of the Goose," Montes de Oca offers a scenic, forested detour full of natural beauty and history. In the Middle Ages, this area was feared for bandits, but today it's a quiet, peaceful stretch where you can appreciate the natural landscape.

Cape Finisterre (Camino Finisterre): Often considered the "end of the world," this cape on the Atlantic is where many pilgrims reflect on their journey. The lighthouse offers incredible ocean views, especially at sunset, and it's a place to take a moment of solitude before returning home.

Santa Catalina de Somoza (Camino Francés): This charming village is a small detour but a true gem with its stone houses, peaceful streets, and the stunning countryside surrounding it. Known for its artisan shops and welcoming atmosphere, it's a great place to take a break and enjoy the simple life of rural Spain.

Local Traditions and Festivals Worth Visiting

Along the Camino, you'll come across towns that come alive during their local festivals. Experiencing these events can add a vibrant layer to your Camino journey, letting you feel the energy of Spanish traditions.

Semana Santa (Holy Week): Throughout Spain, the week leading up to Easter is celebrated with religious processions and ceremonies. In towns like León, Burgos, and Santiago, you'll find Semana Santa processions with elaborate costumes, music, and a deeply spiritual atmosphere.

Fiesta de San Fermín (Pamplona): If your Camino overlaps with early July, make sure to stop in Pamplona for the famous Running of the Bulls. Even if you don't participate, watching the event and enjoying the lively atmosphere is unforgettable. Be aware that accommodation can fill up quickly, so plan ahead.

Feast of St. James (Santiago de Compostela): Celebrated on July 25, this festival honors St. James with fireworks, music, and cultural events throughout Santiago. It's a celebration like no other, as the city becomes alive with energy. If you're lucky enough to arrive during this time, it's a wonderful way to end your pilgrimage.

Magosto Festival (Galicia): Celebrated in November, Magosto is Galicia's chestnut festival. If you're on the Camino during this time, you'll find small villages celebrating with roasted chestnuts, local wine, and music. It's a cozy, community-centered festival that's perfect for experiencing local culture.

Unique Stops for Nature Lovers

For nature enthusiasts, the Camino offers much more than historic sites and cathedrals. The paths are filled with beautiful natural spots, from lush forests to secluded beaches.

Fragas do Eume (Galicia): A short detour for those ending in Santiago, Fragas do Eume is one of Spain's most pristine natural parks, with lush forests, rivers, and trails. It's perfect for a day trip if you want to experience a different side of Galician nature.

Redondela (Camino Portugués): Known for its river views and green landscapes, Redondela offers a refreshing change from the urban stretches of the Camino Portugués. It's a quiet town where you can enjoy riverside walks, scenic bridges, and bird-watching.

Playa de la Salvé (Laredo) (Camino del Norte): Located on the Northern Way, Playa de la Salvé is a long, sandy beach ideal for taking a break. Its golden sands and calm waves make it a great spot for swimming or simply resting with your feet in the sand.

Roncesvalles Forest (Camino Francés): This enchanting forest near the start of the Camino Francés is often mist-covered, creating an almost mystical atmosphere. Walking through its trees and streams can feel like stepping into a storybook.

Artistic and Historical Sights Beyond the Main Route

For art and history lovers, the Camino offers fascinating places just a little off the main route. These stops add a cultural layer that deepens your experience.

Gaudí's Episcopal Palace (Astorga): Designed by the famous architect Antoni Gaudí, this neo-Gothic building in Astorga is a stunning example of his work. Today, it serves as a museum dedicated to the Camino de Santiago, with exhibits on pilgrimage history and artifacts.

Monastery of San Millán de la Cogolla (Camino Francés): Recognized as the birthplace of the Spanish language, this monastery is a UNESCO World Heritage site and houses an incredible collection of manuscripts. It's a bit of a detour, but the monastery's history and architecture make it worthwhile.

Romanesque Church of San Martín de Frómista (Camino Francés): This beautifully preserved church is one of Spain's finest examples of Romanesque architecture. Built in the 11th century, it stands out for its intricate carvings and balanced design.

Cuevas de Altamira (Santillana del Mar) (Camino del Norte): Known for its prehistoric cave paintings, the Altamira Cave is called the "Sistine Chapel of prehistoric art." While the original cave is closed, the nearby museum offers a replica that's worth a visit.

This chapter is your guide to uncovering the lesser-known treasures of the Camino. These hidden gems—

villages, natural spots, festivals, and cultural sites—add depth to the pilgrimage, giving you memories beyond the traditional route. As you travel through these places, take the time to soak up the local atmosphere, meet the people, and appreciate each step of the journey.

Chapter 7: Essential Stops on the Camino: Landmarks and Icons

Walking the Camino de Santiago is as much about the places you pass through as it is about reaching the final destination. Along the way, pilgrims encounter historic churches, natural wonders, and iconic landmarks that deepen the journey's meaning. This chapter explores essential stops on the Camino, from the historic starting point of Saint-Jean-Pied-de-Port to the majestic end in Santiago de Compostela.

Starting Point: Saint-Jean-Pied-de-Port

For those taking the Camino Francés, Saint-Jean-Pied-de-Port in France is where it all begins. Nestled in the foothills of the Pyrenees, this charming town brims with history and is a place for pilgrims to reflect and gather strength for the journey ahead. The main street, Rue de la Citadelle, leads to the town's ancient stone gate, where pilgrims first step onto the Camino path.

In Saint-Jean-Pied-de-Port, you can pick up your Credencial del Peregrino (Pilgrim Passport) at the Pilgrim's Office, which is essential for collecting stamps along the route and ultimately receiving your Compostela certificate in Santiago. The town's fortress, Citadel of Saint-Jean-Pied-de-Port, is worth a visit for its panoramic views of the Pyrenees and its role in French history. Many pilgrims find this town the perfect place to take a moment of gratitude and anticipation before they set off on the long road ahead.

Must-Visit Churches and Cathedrals

The Camino is marked by centuries-old churches and cathedrals that have seen thousands of pilgrims pass by their doors. These buildings are not just places of worship but also monuments to medieval architecture, art, and culture. Here are a few standout locations that deserve your attention:

Santa María la Real in Pamplona: Located in one of Spain's most famous cities, this Gothic-style cathedral offers a glimpse into medieval architecture with its soaring towers and ornate interiors. Don't miss the cloisters and the museum, which features religious art and artifacts from the region.

Burgos Cathedral: Known as one of Spain's most impressive cathedrals, this UNESCO World Heritage site is a masterpiece of Gothic architecture.

With its towering spires, intricate façades, and magnificent interior chapels, Burgos Cathedral is a spiritual highlight of the Camino.

Iglesia de San Martín in Frómista: This Romanesque church is known for its simple elegance and harmonious proportions. Built in the 11th century, Iglesia de San Martín is one of the best-preserved Romanesque churches in Spain, offering a quiet and reflective atmosphere for pilgrims.

• Cathedral of León: Famous for its stunning stained-glass windows, the Cathedral of León is a must-see stop. This Gothic cathedral, often compared to those in Paris, lets in a kaleidoscope of colors that adds a magical quality to the space. Pilgrims can explore the cloisters, museum, and ornate carvings that cover this iconic site.

Each church and cathedral offers a moment of pause and reflection, with centuries of history captured in their walls. Visiting these sacred spaces connects you with the generations of pilgrims who've come before.

Famous Bridges and Historic Sites

Throughout the Camino, pilgrims cross ancient bridges and encounter historic sites that connect the past to the present. Each bridge has its story, marking moments of architectural skill and serving as a reminder of the people who traveled these roads long before us.

Puente la Reina: Known as the "Bridge of the Queen," this medieval bridge spans the Arga River and is an architectural gem. Built in the 11th century, the bridge's arches and symmetry reflect Romanesque design and have welcomed pilgrims for centuries. Walking across this bridge feels like stepping back in time.

Bridge of San Nicolás de Puente Fitero: Located near Nájera, this bridge is famous for its link to the Order of Saint John of Jerusalem, an order of knights who protected pilgrims. Today, it remains an emblem of the Camino's long-standing tradition of hospitality and protection.

Roman Bridge in Cacabelos: This small town is known for its charming Roman bridge, which crosses the Cúa River. It's a simple yet picturesque stop, perfect for a moment of rest by the riverbank and a reminder of the Camino's ancient origins.

These bridges symbolize both the challenges and connections of the Camino, bridging past and present and linking pilgrims to centuries-old traditions.

Natural Wonders: Forests, Rivers, and Mountains

The Camino is renowned for its landscapes, which change with each region. From the peaks of the Pyrenees to the lush forests of Galicia, the natural wonders along the Camino bring a sense of peace and inspiration to those walking the path.

The Pyrenees: The first major challenge for many pilgrims, the Pyrenees Mountains mark the beginning of the Camino Francés. The ascent is steep, but the views are breathtaking, with mist-covered peaks and lush valleys that set the tone for the journey.

Irati Forest: Near Roncesvalles, this forest offers a tranquil escape, with towering trees and shaded paths that provide relief after the climb over the Pyrenees. Known for its diversity of wildlife, the Irati Forest is a reminder of the beauty of untouched nature.

The Meseta: This flat, arid plateau stretches across central Spain and offers a different kind of beauty. The Meseta's expansive views, wheat fields, and endless skies provide a sense of calm and reflection, encouraging pilgrims to focus inward as they walk.

Galicia's Eucalyptus Forests: As pilgrims near the end of the journey, they enter Galicia, a region known for its dense eucalyptus forests. The smell of eucalyptus fills the air, adding a fresh, invigorating element to the final stretch. These forests, often shrouded in mist, feel almost magical and offer a perfect setting for the Camino's closing days.

Nature on the Camino is both a challenge and a blessing, with each landscape bringing its own rhythm and lessons.

Santiago de Compostela: The End of the Journey

After hundreds of miles and countless experiences, pilgrims finally arrive in Santiago de Compostela, where the journey culminates at the Cathedral of Santiago. This majestic cathedral, dedicated to Saint James, is a marvel of Romanesque, Gothic, and Baroque architecture, standing as a symbol of faith, endurance, and accomplishment.

Upon arrival, pilgrims often participate in the Pilgrim's Mass, held daily at noon, where the Botafumeiro, a giant incense burner, swings through the cathedral's nave. This ancient ceremony celebrates the arrival of pilgrims and serves as a moving finale to the journey. For many, receiving the Compostela, a certificate of completion, is a meaningful moment, symbolizing the hard work, resilience, and dedication poured into the walk.

Santiago itself is a vibrant city, filled with lively squares, narrow medieval streets, and bustling markets. Pilgrims can explore the city's historic quarter, enjoy local cuisine, and reflect on their journey with fellow travelers. Santiago de Compostela isn't just the end of a physical path; it's a place where many pilgrims find a new beginning, whether that's a fresh perspective, a renewed sense of purpose, or simply a feeling of peace.

From start to finish, the Camino is a walk through history, spirituality, and natural beauty. Each stop along the way, whether a historic bridge or a quiet forest, brings something to the journey. For those embarking on this adventure, these essential stops serve as milestones, reminding you of the path you've chosen and the countless pilgrims who've walked it before.

Chapter 8: Pilgrim Etiquette and Camino Culture

Walking the Camino de Santiago isn't just about covering miles—it's about joining a living tradition filled with shared respect, cultural customs, and a spirit that has drawn people from all backgrounds for centuries. Understanding the unique etiquette and customs of the Camino can enhance your experience, help you build meaningful connections, and ensure that you leave a positive impact along the way.

Camino Customs and Local Traditions

The Camino has a rich tapestry of customs and local traditions that have developed over centuries. From unique greetings to pilgrim rituals, embracing these customs can deepen your connection to the journey. One of the first things you'll notice is the traditional pilgrim greeting, "Buen Camino" (meaning "Good Camino"), shared among travelers along the route. This simple phrase captures a spirit of encouragement and solidarity, reminding you that you're part of a community all heading toward Santiago.

As you walk through villages and towns, you'll come across albergues (pilgrim hostels) that operate on a first-come, first-served basis and often involve shared sleeping spaces. Respecting these spaces by being considerate of quiet hours and keeping communal areas tidy is a basic yet essential part of pilgrim etiquette. The Camino also has its own rituals, like collecting stamps in your credencial (pilgrim passport) at each stop along the way. These stamps become a cherished record of your journey and are essential for receiving your Compostela certificate in Santiago.

Another long-standing tradition involves carrying a scallop shell—the symbol of the Camino—on your backpack. This shell has been a pilgrim symbol for centuries and serves as a reminder of the journey's purpose, while also helping other pilgrims recognize you as a fellow traveler.

Respecting Fellow Pilgrims and Locals

The Camino brings people from all walks of life together, and respecting the diversity of those around you is vital. Pilgrims come from different cultures, age groups, and personal backgrounds, and every pilgrim has their own pace, reasons, and goals for walking. Being considerate means respecting both their space and personal journey. A simple smile, a warm greeting, or a kind word can go a long way in fostering the supportive atmosphere that makes the Camino special.

Respect also extends to the local residents who welcome pilgrims into their towns. Some locals have been connected to the Camino for generations, opening their homes, offering food, and maintaining the paths. Treating them with kindness, learning a few basic phrases in Spanish, and showing gratitude for their hospitality honors their role in keeping the Camino alive.

The Camino can be challenging, especially when shared spaces become crowded. Practicing patience, waiting your turn in queues, and offering a hand to someone who might need help are simple ways to keep the atmosphere positive. Respect for others is what makes the Camino feel like a shared experience, not just a solo journey.

Understanding the Spirit of the Camino

The Camino has a unique spirit rooted in pilgrimage, spirituality, and personal transformation. While everyone's journey is personal, understanding this spirit can add a deeper layer to your experience. Many pilgrims find that walking the Camino fosters a sense of humility and gratitude, as they leave behind everyday conveniences for a simpler, more mindful way of living. Embracing this spirit means letting go of comparisons, slowing down, and allowing each day to unfold as it comes.

It's also common to face challenges—whether physical, emotional, or logistical—that bring out resilience and patience. Pilgrims often experience a profound sense of calm and purpose as they walk, and many find themselves reflecting on life, relationships, and their personal goals. Whether you're walking for spiritual reasons or simply for the adventure, keeping an open mind and embracing each moment can reveal new insights and a sense of peace that makes the Camino truly transformative.

Building Connections: Meeting Fellow Travelers

The Camino is known for creating connections among people who might otherwise never cross paths. Whether you're sharing a meal, walking alongside someone for a few kilometers, or helping someone carry their bag, these encounters often lead to friendships and memorable conversations. Many pilgrims find that the people they meet are as impactful as the journey itself.

Approaching the Camino with openness allows you to experience the camaraderie that the route is famous for. Some days, you might walk in silence, but other times, a friendly chat with a stranger can brighten the miles.

Bonds formed on the Camino often last a lifetime, as shared challenges and victories bring people closer. Exchanging stories, sharing a laugh, or even supporting each other during difficult moments adds to the spirit of the Camino and makes it feel like a communal experience.

Giving Back to the Camino Community

The Camino community is sustained by a network of people, from local volunteers to fellow pilgrims, who give back to keep the Camino thriving. Once you've experienced the Camino, you might feel compelled to contribute in your own way. Many former pilgrims choose to volunteer at albergues, help maintain the paths, or support new pilgrims with advice and encouragement.

Another way to give back is by supporting local businesses and albergues that serve the Camino community. Purchasing goods from local shops, dining at family-owned restaurants, or donating to small, community-run albergues can make a big difference to the people who depend on the pilgrimage. Giving back doesn't have to be grand; even small acts of kindness, like picking up litter along the trail or offering water to a fellow pilgrim, contribute to the positive, supportive environment that makes the Camino special.

The Camino de Santiago is more than a journey; it's a living tradition where respect, connection, and a shared sense of purpose create a unique experience. By understanding the customs, respecting those around you, and embracing the Camino's spirit, you become part of something much larger than yourself. Each step is not only a move toward Santiago but a chance to connect with people, places, and a tradition that has endured for centuries.

Chapter 9. Challenges and Rewards of the Camino

The Camino de Santiago is more than just a long walk through Spain; it's a journey that pushes you physically, mentally, and emotionally. Many pilgrims come with high hopes, only to find that walking day after day brings up challenges they hadn't anticipated. But facing these challenges and pushing through them is where the real magic of the Camino happens. In this chapter, we'll explore the common challenges you might face, practical ways to manage them, and the incredible rewards that come from completing this journey.

Physical Challenges: Terrain, Weather, and Fatigue

The Camino de Santiago covers a diverse landscape, each region with its own unique terrain and weather patterns. Here are some of the main physical challenges you're likely to encounter:

Terrain: The Camino routes vary from smooth, paved city streets to rugged mountain paths. On the Camino Francés, for example, the Pyrenees Mountains can be steep and challenging at the beginning. Further along, the flat, open plains of the Meseta can be monotonous and mentally draining. In contrast, the Camino del Norte has hilly coastal paths that demand more stamina and careful footing. Preparing for these varied terrains by doing training walks with similar terrain at home will help build your confidence and endurance.

Weather: The weather on the Camino can be unpredictable, no matter the season. Summer months may bring scorching heat, especially on the Meseta, where shade is sparse, while spring and autumn can surprise you with rain, muddy paths, or even cold nights. The Northern routes may experience fog and rain more often. Preparing for different weather by bringing versatile gear, such as a rain poncho, layers, and quick-dry clothing, will go a long way.

Fatigue: Walking up to 20-30 kilometers a day isn't easy, especially over weeks. Physical fatigue is a common experience, with sore muscles, aching feet, and blistered toes becoming part of the daily routine. One way to manage fatigue is by listening to your body, taking breaks as needed, and adjusting your pace.

Regular stretching, a well-fitted backpack, and proper footwear make a huge difference, as does keeping yourself hydrated and well-nourished with healthy snacks and meals.

Mental and Emotional Challenges

Aside from the physical aspects, the Camino is a test of mental strength. After a week or two on the road, the novelty of the journey can wear off, leaving you with only your thoughts and the sound of your own footsteps. This can lead to feelings of loneliness, boredom, and even doubt about whether you can complete the journey. Here's how to prepare for and handle these mental and emotional challenges:

Loneliness: While many pilgrims start the Camino to experience solitude, the long hours of walking can sometimes lead to unexpected feelings of loneliness, especially if you're a solo traveler. One way to combat this is by joining others for meals, striking up conversations with fellow pilgrims along the way, or staying in albergues (pilgrim hostels), where socializing is part of the experience. Even a few minutes of connection with others can lift your spirits.

Boredom: Spending hours each day doing the same thing can feel repetitive. To keep your mind engaged, you can listen to audiobooks, podcasts, or music while you walk. Journaling about your thoughts and experiences each night can also help you process the journey. Embrace the opportunity for a break from the busyness of daily life and let yourself appreciate the simple act of walking.

Doubt and Self-Criticism: Some days, the walk can feel impossible, and you may start doubting your ability to finish or question why you started in the first place. When these feelings come up, remember that they're a normal part of the journey. Many pilgrims feel this way, especially when they hit the "Camino Wall." Taking things one step at a time, instead of focusing on the total distance ahead, can help you stay grounded and motivated.

How to Overcome the "Camino Wall"

The "Camino Wall" is a term used by many pilgrims to describe the physical and mental barrier they hit around the midway point. It's when you feel exhausted, unmotivated, and ready to give up. Getting through the wall can be one of the most challenging parts of the Camino, but it's also one of the most rewarding.

Pace Yourself: Don't feel pressured to keep up with other pilgrims. Everyone has their own pace, and pushing yourself too hard can lead to burnout or injury. Slow down, take shorter walking days if needed, and remind yourself that rest is part of the journey.

Celebrate Small Wins: Each day you complete is a small victory. Give yourself credit for what you've accomplished, whether it's climbing a difficult hill, dealing with a rainy day, or simply getting out of bed and walking.

Keep Your Goal in Sight: When the going gets tough, remember why you chose to walk the Camino in the first place. Visualize the moment you'll arrive in Santiago and stand before the cathedral, knowing you've completed a journey few others have. This mental image can help keep you focused and inspired to keep going.

The Rewards of Completing the Camino

The rewards of the Camino go far beyond reaching Santiago. While arriving at the cathedral in Santiago is the pinnacle of the journey, the experiences, memories, and friendships you gain along the way are just as meaningful. Here are some of the rewards you'll likely experience:

A Sense of Accomplishment: Completing the Camino, whether you've walked 100 kilometers or 800, is a major achievement. It's a reminder of your own resilience and capability, something you can carry with you for years to come.

New Friendships: The Camino brings people from all around the world together. Sharing meals, walking together, and helping each other through difficult times creates a strong bond. Many pilgrims say the friendships they make are one of the best parts of the experience.

Personal Growth and Reflection: The Camino offers a rare chance for deep reflection. Away from the noise of daily life, many pilgrims find clarity on their personal struggles, goals, and dreams. The Camino has a way of stripping away the unnecessary, allowing you to connect with what really matters.

Connection to Nature and Simplicity: Walking day after day through fields, forests, and mountains brings you closer to nature and a simpler way of life. Many pilgrims come away with a renewed appreciation for nature, silence, and the beauty of slowing down.

Lessons Learned on the Camino

The Camino is more than a physical path; it's a journey that teaches valuable lessons that you'll carry into your life long after returning home. Some lessons that many pilgrims learn include:

Patience and Acceptance: The Camino teaches you to accept things you can't control, like the weather, sore feet, or limited options for food and lodging. It's a reminder that sometimes, the only thing you can change is your attitude.

Trust in the Journey: The Camino has a way of working out, even when things seem uncertain. Whether it's a stranger offering a kind word or an albergue with one last bed available, many pilgrims come to trust that the path provides.

Living with Less: Carrying everything you need on your back shows you how little you truly need to be content. This minimalist mindset often carries over into daily life, encouraging a focus on experiences and relationships over material possessions.

The Power of Perseverance: Every pilgrim faces moments of doubt and fatigue, yet they push on. Completing the Camino is a reminder that we're stronger than we think and that with patience and determination, we can reach our goals.

The Camino de Santiago offers many rewards, but not without its challenges. As you face each step, remember that every struggle brings growth, and every mile walked is an achievement. Embrace both the highs and lows, as they are part of what makes the Camino a life-changing experience.

Chapter 10: Health and Safety on the Camino

Health and safety are vital to ensuring your Camino journey is comfortable, manageable, and enjoyable. The Camino is an incredible experience, but the physical demands of daily walking, the unpredictability of weather, and the potential for minor injuries mean it's important to prioritize your well-being. From staying hydrated to handling unexpected emergencies, here's everything you need to know to stay safe and healthy on the trail.

Staying Hydrated and Healthy on the Trail

Walking for hours each day under various weather conditions means keeping your body well-hydrated is essential. Proper hydration not only helps maintain energy levels but also prevents heat exhaustion, headaches, and muscle cramps.

Hydration Tips:

Drink Regularly: Carry a water bottle or hydration pack and sip frequently rather than gulping down large amounts at once. Aim for at least 2-3 liters per day, depending on weather conditions and your body's needs.

Check for Refilling Points: Most towns and villages along the Camino have fountains where you can refill your water bottle. Look for signs indicating potable water ("agua potable"). It's a good idea to carry a spare bottle if you're passing through a stretch without water points.

Electrolytes: Walking for long periods can lead to electrolyte loss through sweat. Carry electrolyte tablets or powder to add to your water for a quick boost, especially on hotter days.

Stay Aware of Your Body's Signals: Feeling lightheaded, fatigued, or having a dry mouth can be signs of dehydration. Listen to your body and rest if you feel these symptoms.

Eating well is just as important as staying hydrated. The Camino offers plenty of food options, but planning for healthy snacks and balanced meals will support your stamina.

Nutrition Tips:

Eat Balanced Meals: Opt for the traditional "Pilgrim's Menu" whenever possible, as it's usually affordable and includes a starter, main dish, and dessert. These meals provide the protein, carbs, and fats needed to refuel.

Carry Snacks: Pack light snacks like nuts, dried fruit, or energy bars for when you're between towns or on a longer stretch.

Avoid Overeating: While it's tempting to indulge, eating too much can make you sluggish. Keep meals balanced and nutritious to maintain a steady energy level.

Preventing and Treating Blisters

Blisters are one of the most common issues pilgrims face on the Camino. Even with good shoes, the repetitive motion of walking long distances can create friction that leads to blisters, especially on hot days or rough terrain. Preventing them from developing, and treating them properly if they do, is key to keeping your feet in good shape.

Preventing Blisters:

Wear Well-Fitted Shoes: Shoes that fit well are your first line of defense. Avoid shoes that are too tight or too loose, as both can cause friction.

Ensure they are well broken-in before you start your Camino.

Use High-Quality Socks: Moisture-wicking socks, preferably made of merino wool or a synthetic blend, help keep your feet dry. Some pilgrims use two pairs of socks (a thin liner sock and a thicker outer sock) to reduce friction.

Apply Lubricant: Products like Vaseline or blister prevention creams can be applied to areas prone to friction, such as the heels and balls of your feet. This extra layer helps minimize chafing.

Keep Feet Dry: Moisture makes skin softer and more susceptible to blisters. Change your socks if they become damp, and take off your shoes during breaks to let your feet air out.

Treating Blisters:

Clean the Area: If you do develop a blister, keep it clean to prevent infection. Use antiseptic wipes or a mild soap and water.

Drain Carefully: If the blister is large and painful, you may need to drain it. Use a sterile needle to pierce the side and let the fluid out, but avoid removing the skin, as it acts as a natural barrier.

Cover and Protect: Use a blister pad, moleskin, or gauze to protect the area. Bandages should be changed daily or whenever they become wet. Some pilgrims swear by Compeed blister pads, which provide cushioning and help prevent further rubbing.

Taking good care of your feet can mean the difference between a smooth journey and painful struggles. If you feel "hot spots" developing, stop immediately and address them before they turn into full-blown blisters.

Safety Tips for Solo Travelers

Traveling the Camino solo can be incredibly rewarding, offering time for personal reflection and independence. However, it's wise to keep some safety tips in mind, especially if you're traveling alone.

Stick to Popular Routes:

The Camino Francés is the most popular and well-marked route, with plenty of pilgrims and support services. Solo travelers often feel safer on this route, as it offers more consistent company and accessible resources.

Stay Connected:

Share your daily itinerary with friends or family back home. Regularly update them on your progress, especially if you plan to veer off the main routes.

Consider carrying a basic phone or even a GPS device in case of emergencies. Most towns have Wi-Fi, and Spain has good cell coverage along the Camino.

Trust Your Instincts:

If something doesn't feel right, trust your gut. Walk with a group if you're uncomfortable with certain areas or situations.

Avoid walking alone at night or in isolated areas. Most pilgrims walk during the day and stay in town or albergue accommodations by evening.

Be Cautious with Valuables:

Pickpocketing is rare but not unheard of. Keep your valuables in a secure money belt or a hidden pocket, and never leave them unattended.

When staying in shared dormitories, use a small lock for your backpack or valuables.

Walking alone is safe for most travelers, especially on the more popular paths. However, staying aware of your surroundings and taking a few precautions will ensure you feel secure and confident along the way.

Dealing with Emergencies and First Aid

Even with careful preparation, emergencies can happen, from unexpected injuries to sudden illnesses. Knowing how to handle them and where to find help can make a big difference in these situations.

Know When to Seek Help:

Minor Injuries: For small scrapes, blisters, or strains, carry a basic first-aid kit with bandages, antiseptic wipes, pain relief medication, and blister pads.

Serious Injuries: If you experience a serious injury, seek medical assistance immediately. The emergency number in Spain is 112, which connects you to police, fire, or medical help.

First Aid Tips:

Sprains and Strains: Rest the affected area, apply ice if possible, and elevate it. Avoid continuing your walk if you're experiencing significant pain, as it could worsen the injury.

Dehydration and Heat Exhaustion: Rest in the shade, drink water, and cool your body with a damp cloth. Severe dehydration may require medical attention.

Stomach Upsets: Travelers often experience digestive issues due to new foods, water changes, or exhaustion. Carry anti-diarrheal medication and hydrate if you experience any stomach discomfort.

Medical Centers and Pharmacies:

Pharmacies (farmacias) are available in most towns along the Camino and are well-stocked with basic medical supplies and over-the-counter medications. The pharmacists are generally knowledgeable and can provide help for minor issues.

In case of more serious health concerns, ask your albergue host or a fellow pilgrim for guidance to the nearest clinic or hospital. Major cities along the Camino have hospitals equipped to handle emergencies.

A basic knowledge of first aid and knowing where to get help can make a big difference. Don't hesitate to seek assistance if you're feeling unwell or injured; taking care of your health is your top priority on this journey.

Managing Sun Exposure and Insect Bites

Sun exposure can be intense on the Camino, especially during summer. Coupled with the occasional presence of mosquitoes and other insects, it's worth taking some extra steps to protect yourself.

Sun Protection:

Sunscreen: Apply broad-spectrum sunscreen with an SPF of at least 30 in the morning, and reapply every two hours, especially on exposed areas like the neck, face, and arms.

Headwear and Clothing: A wide-brimmed hat or cap and lightweight, long-sleeve clothing provide excellent sun protection. Choose breathable fabrics to stay comfortable in the heat.

Seek Shade: Take advantage of shaded areas whenever possible, especially during midday, when the sun is strongest.

Insect Protection:

Use Insect Repellent: A DEET-based repellent is effective for keeping mosquitoes and other bugs away, especially in the evening or near rivers.

Avoid Stagnant Water: Mosquitoes are often found around stagnant water, so be mindful of where you rest or set up for a break.

Treat Bites Promptly: If you do get bitten, applying an anti-itch cream or aloe vera gel can soothe the skin and prevent irritation. Avoid scratching bites, as this can lead to infection.

Taking small steps to protect yourself from sun and insect exposure will go a long way in keeping you comfortable and focused on your journey.

In this chapter, we've covered practical tips for staying healthy and safe on the Camino. From keeping hydrated and preventing blisters to handling emergencies and staying sun-safe, these guidelines will help you walk confidently each day. Health and safety are key to enjoying the Camino experience, so prepare well, listen to your body, and make adjustments as needed to keep your journey rewarding and worry-free.

Chapter 11: Camino de Santiago for Beginners

The Camino de Santiago has a unique pull for travelers, whether they're seeking personal growth, an active adventure, or simply a way to experience the rich culture of Spain. If you're a beginner, the Camino may feel overwhelming, but with some preparation, it can be a rewarding journey for all ages, fitness levels, and backgrounds. This chapter is dedicated to helping first-time pilgrims make the most of their Camino experience, covering everything from pre-trip preparations to tips tailored for solo travelers, families, and groups.

Preparing for Your First Camino

Walking the Camino de Santiago is not just a physical journey; it's an experience that requires mental and emotional preparation. Here's a guide to what beginners need to consider:

Choose Your Route Wisely: The Camino is not a single path but a network of routes that converge in Santiago. Popular options include the Camino Francés (French Way), which is well-marked and has ample facilities, making it ideal for beginners. The Camino Portugués (Portuguese Way) offers a coastal experience, while the Camino del Norte (Northern Way) is scenic but more challenging. Research each route to find the one that aligns with your fitness level, time available, and interests.

Plan Your Timeline and Daily Distance: Most beginners opt to cover 20-25 kilometers (12-15 miles) per day, a manageable distance that allows time for breaks and exploration. The full Camino Francés takes around 30-35 days, but many beginners choose to walk the last 100 kilometers from Sarria, which can be done in about a week.

Training and Physical Preparation: The Camino isn't a race, but a certain level of fitness will make your journey more enjoyable. Start walking regularly a few months before your trip, gradually increasing your distance and carrying a backpack similar to what you'll bring on the Camino. Include hills and rough terrain to prepare for the varying landscapes.

Pack Lightly and Strategically: As a beginner, it's tempting to overpack, but remember that you'll carry everything on your back. Aim for a backpack that weighs no more than 10% of your body weight. Essentials include comfortable, broken-in hiking boots, lightweight clothing, a small first-aid kit, water, and a rain jacket or poncho.

Secure Your Accommodations: While many pilgrims walk without pre-booking, beginners may find it reassuring to reserve accommodations in key towns, especially during peak seasons. This ensures you have a place to stay after a long day of walking. Many albergues (pilgrim hostels) allow reservations, especially for private rooms or beds in smaller villages.

Mindset and Expectations: The Camino is physically demanding, but mental preparation is just as important. Expect to face challenges, from weather changes to fatigue and homesickness. Embrace the idea of flexibility and be open to the journey unfolding in its own way, rather than sticking rigidly to a set plan.

Preparing ahead allows you to enjoy the Camino with less stress and more energy for each day's adventure.

Tips for Solo Travelers, Families, and Groups

The Camino welcomes a diverse mix of pilgrims, and whether you're going solo, with family, or as part of a group, there are ways to make the most of the experience.

For Solo Travelers:

Safety and Community: Walking alone might sound intimidating, but the Camino is one of the safest routes for solo travelers. The well-marked trails, abundance of pilgrims, and welcoming albergues provide a sense of community. Many solo travelers find companionship naturally along the way.

Embrace Your Independence: Walking solo allows you to set your own pace, stop as often as you like, and focus on personal reflection. Carry essentials like a small first-aid kit, phone with emergency contacts, and a power bank for peace of mind.

Social Opportunities: Solo pilgrims often make friends in albergues or over communal meals, forming "Camino families" of people who walk together for several days or even weeks. Don't hesitate to introduce yourself or join group dinners, as the Camino is full of fellow pilgrims eager to connect.

For Families:

Adjust Your Daily Distances: If you're traveling with children, plan shorter daily distances, perhaps 10-15 kilometers, to make the experience enjoyable for everyone. Take plenty of breaks and keep snacks on hand to maintain energy levels.

Involve Kids in the Planning: Older children can participate in planning and packing, making them feel more involved and excited. Teaching them basic phrases in Spanish or sharing stories about the Camino's history can deepen their experience.

Choose Family-Friendly Accommodation: Not all albergues cater to families, so consider booking private rooms or choosing hotels in some areas to ensure everyone gets a good night's sleep. Family-friendly albergues are often quieter and have amenities suited to young children.

Activities for Kids: Bring simple activities like travel journals, coloring books, or a camera. Kids often enjoy collecting stamps in their pilgrim credentials, turning the journey into a memorable adventure.

For Groups:

Set Group Expectations: When traveling in a group, it's essential to agree on daily goals, rest times, and meal plans. Each person will have their own pace, so consider allowing members to walk solo for parts of the day and meet at designated stops.

Communication is Key: Decide on a communication plan if you separate, such as checking in at rest points or sending text messages. A group itinerary can help keep everyone on the same page.

Divide Responsibilities: Consider assigning each member tasks, such as navigation, meal planning, or first aid, to streamline decision-making. This can foster teamwork and reduce stress.

Whether you're a solo adventurer or traveling with loved ones, the Camino offers a flexible experience that can be tailored to any group size.

Advice for Older and Less Experienced Hikers

Age and experience shouldn't deter you from the Camino. Many older pilgrims and those new to hiking successfully complete the journey each year. Here are some tips for making it enjoyable:

Pace Yourself: Start slow, especially in the first few days, to avoid overexertion. Walking at a comfortable pace helps prevent injury and allows you to adjust to the physical demands of the Camino.

Use Walking Poles: Walking poles provide stability, reduce impact on knees and joints, and are especially helpful on uneven terrain. Many older pilgrims swear by them, and they can make a significant difference in endurance.

Consider Baggage Transfer Services: Some companies offer luggage transfer between accommodations, which can ease the physical burden of carrying a heavy pack. It's a great option for older walkers or those with limited strength.

Take Rest Days: Unlike faster-paced hikers, older or less experienced pilgrims benefit from rest days. Plan a break every few days to recover, explore local towns, and enjoy the experience at a relaxed pace.

Listen to Your Body: Rest if you feel pain or fatigue, and don't hesitate to shorten your daily distance if needed. The Camino isn't a race, and there's no shame in taking it slowly. Many older pilgrims find the slower pace allows them to soak in the beauty and enjoy a more reflective experience.

With a bit of adaptation, older and less experienced hikers can complete the Camino with joy and comfort, proving that the journey is accessible to everyone.

Common Mistakes to Avoid on the Camino

Even well-prepared pilgrims make mistakes. Here's a list of common pitfalls and how to avoid them:

Overpacking: It's easy to think you need every possible item, but a heavy backpack can wear you out quickly. Pack only the essentials and remember that you can buy supplies along the way if needed.

Not Breaking in Footwear: New shoes or boots are a recipe for blisters. Walk in your footwear for at least a few weeks before starting the Camino, and wear moisture-wicking socks to keep feet dry.

Skipping Stretching and Rest: Walking long distances without proper stretching can lead to muscle strain. Take a few minutes each morning and evening to stretch, especially focusing on legs and back.

Underestimating the Weather: Spain's weather can be unpredictable. Carry a lightweight rain jacket, wear layers for cold mornings, and bring a hat or sunscreen for sunny days.

Ignoring Hydration and Nutrition: Staying hydrated is critical, especially in warmer weather. Carry a water bottle and refill it regularly. Pack high-energy snacks, like nuts or granola bars, for quick boosts throughout the day.

Forgetting Rest Days: Many pilgrims think they need to walk every day, but rest days prevent burnout. Use rest days to explore towns, do laundry, and give your muscles a break.

Pushing Through Injuries: Blisters, muscle strains, and other minor injuries can worsen if ignored. Listen to your body and take care of minor issues before they become bigger problems. There are pharmacies in most towns along the Camino where you can buy supplies like bandages and blister treatments.

By avoiding these common mistakes, you'll increase your chances of having a comfortable, enjoyable journey on the Camino.

The Camino de Santiago is an incredible experience for beginners, families, solo travelers, and groups alike. With the right preparation and mindset, anyone can embrace the journey and enjoy each step of this historic pilgrimage.

Chapter 12: Special Camino Experiences

Walking the Camino de Santiago is not only about reaching a destination; it's about embracing a journey filled with meaning, rituals, and experiences that connect you to centuries of tradition. Many pilgrims find that these unique elements deepen their connection to the Camino and provide opportunities for spiritual reflection, personal insight, and unforgettable memories. This chapter explores some of the special experiences that make the Camino so much more than just a long walk.

The "Credencial del Peregrino" (Pilgrim Passport)

One of the first things every pilgrim receives is the Credencial del Peregrino, or Pilgrim Passport. This small, foldable booklet is much more than a piece of paper—it's your proof of pilgrimage, a memento of your journey, and a key to many experiences along the Camino.

Your Credencial serves several purposes. Most importantly, it's a record that proves you walked the required distance to earn your Compostela in Santiago, especially the last 100 kilometers if you're on foot (or 200 kilometers if biking or on horseback). Along the way, you'll collect stamps at albergues, churches, cafes, and other stops. Each stamp tells a story, capturing the places, people, and moments that mark your path to Santiago. It's a visual diary of your journey and becomes a cherished keepsake when you return home.

How to Get Your Credencial:

Before You Arrive: Some pilgrims obtain their Credencial from Camino associations in their home countries. These groups often send it to you by mail for a small donation, which helps support Camino infrastructure.

Upon Arrival: Many pilgrims pick up their Credencial at the start of their journey. Major starting points, like Saint-Jean-Pied-de-Port, Roncesvalles, and Pamplona, offer Credenciales at pilgrim offices, churches, or albergues.

The Credencial is an integral part of the Camino experience. It transforms each day into a series of milestones, reminding you of the progress you've made and the journey that still lies ahead.

Collecting Stamps and Earning Your Compostela

Collecting stamps, or sellos, along the Camino is one of the most beloved traditions for pilgrims. Every time you stop for the night, visit a church, or pause at a cafe, you have an opportunity to gather a new stamp in your Credencial. These stamps are more than just proof of your journey; they're symbols of each place, some beautifully designed and unique to their location.

Where to Get Stamps:

Albergues and Hostels: Almost every albergue offers stamps for pilgrims. Some even have custom designs reflecting the albergue's personality or the town's heritage.

Churches and Cathedrals: Many churches, especially the small village ones, provide stamps. Stopping at these churches allows you to pause, reflect, and experience the sacred history surrounding the Camino.

Cafes and Restaurants: Some cafes, especially those popular with pilgrims, offer stamps for those who stop in for a meal or coffee.

Tourist Information Centers: Many towns along the route have tourist offices where you can get a stamp, especially if they don't have albergues open.

Earning Your Compostela:

When you reach Santiago, you can present your Credencial at the Pilgrim's Office to receive your Compostela, an official certificate of completion. To qualify, you'll need at least two stamps per day from the final 100 kilometers, typically starting in Sarria if you're on the Camino Francés. Your Compostela serves as a reminder of your journey and your personal commitment to reach Santiago.

The act of collecting stamps and earning your Compostela transforms the journey into a series of achievements, where each stamp marks your determination, effort, and connection to the path traveled by pilgrims for centuries.

Experiencing the Botafumeiro in Santiago Cathedral

One of the most iconic experiences for pilgrims arriving in Santiago de Compostela is witnessing the Botafumeiro in Santiago Cathedral. The Botafumeiro, a large ceremonial incense burner, is a marvel of artistry and tradition, suspended from the cathedral ceiling and swung across the nave by a team of skilled attendants known as tiraboleiros. Weighing over 50 kilograms, it reaches heights of 20 meters, filling the cathedral with a rich, smoky aroma.

The Botafumeiro has historical roots in the Camino tradition. Originally, it was used to purify the air due to the crowds of pilgrims who, after weeks of walking, would arrive without access to frequent bathing. Today, it serves as a symbol of welcome and reverence, adding a powerful spiritual touch to the pilgrim's journey.

How to See the Botafumeiro:

Schedule: The Botafumeiro is typically used during special pilgrim masses, held on certain holy days, and on Fridays at 7:30 PM (though times may vary).

Arrive Early: The cathedral fills up quickly, so it's best to arrive at least an hour in advance to get a good spot. Standing near the front or along the sides of the nave provides the best view.

Private Events: Some groups arrange for the Botafumeiro to be swung for private pilgrim gatherings. These events are rare, but if you're walking with a larger group, you may be able to inquire about this option.

Experiencing the Botafumeiro is often described as awe-inspiring and deeply emotional, a final blessing that marks the end of the physical journey and the beginning of a new chapter in life.

Spiritual and Reflective Activities

The Camino is a unique opportunity for spiritual growth, regardless of your personal beliefs. Throughout the pilgrimage, you'll encounter many chances to engage in reflective activities that add depth and meaning to each step. Here are a few popular ways pilgrims connect spiritually on the Camino:

Pilgrim Masses: Many towns and villages along the Camino hold daily pilgrim masses, inviting walkers to come together for blessings, reflection, and gratitude. These masses are non-denominational, often conducted in multiple languages to include all who attend. It's a quiet time to center yourself, give thanks, and reflect on the journey's challenges and rewards.

Lighting Candles: Many churches offer candle-lighting areas where you can light a candle in remembrance or for a personal intention. This simple act of lighting a candle can be a powerful moment of reflection, especially if done in a place that holds significance along the Camino.

Writing in Pilgrim Journals: In some albergues, you'll find pilgrim journals where walkers share their thoughts, reflections, and experiences. Writing in these journals allows you to connect with other pilgrims, both those who have walked before you and those who will follow. Reading the entries from past pilgrims can also offer comfort, wisdom, and encouragement.

Engaging in these activities enhances the Camino experience, grounding your journey in personal meaning and adding a layer of spirituality that resonates with many pilgrims.

Opportunities for Meditation and Contemplation

For many, the Camino is a rare chance to disconnect from the fast pace of everyday life and embrace a slower, more reflective rhythm. Walking for hours each day, surrounded by nature, history, and culture, naturally lends itself to moments of meditation and contemplation. Here are a few ways to incorporate mindfulness and reflection into your journey:

Walking Meditation: The Camino's repetitive rhythm of walking provides an ideal setting for walking meditation. This practice involves focusing on each step, feeling the ground beneath your feet, and being fully present in the moment. Some pilgrims find that this mindful approach helps them stay calm, reduce stress, and feel more connected to the path.

Morning or Evening Reflections: Each day on the Camino offers new experiences, challenges, and insights. Taking a few minutes in the morning to set an intention or at night to reflect on the day can bring clarity and appreciation to your journey. Journaling about these reflections can also serve as a personal record of your inner journey.

Forest Bathing: Inspired by the Japanese practice of shinrin-yoku (forest bathing), spending quiet time in nature can be a profound way to reconnect with yourself and the world around you. The Camino routes pass through stunning forests, valleys, and natural landscapes that invite you to pause, breathe, and simply be present in nature.

Finding Quiet Spots for Meditation: Many places along the Camino are perfect for a quiet pause. Whether it's a secluded chapel, a hilltop view, or a forest clearing, taking time to sit in silence can deepen your connection to the journey and provide a space for inner peace.

Meditation and contemplation on the Camino don't require specific techniques or rituals—simply being mindful of your surroundings and open to the experience creates a natural space for reflection.

In Special Camino Experiences, the heart of the Camino de Santiago is brought to life. These moments and rituals turn the Camino into more than a walk; they transform it into a journey that touches both body and soul. From collecting stamps in your Credencial del Peregrino to experiencing the Botafumeiro in Santiago Cathedral, every tradition, every moment of reflection, and every interaction along the way adds to the richness of the Camino. These experiences connect you to a long line of pilgrims who have walked this path before, creating memories and personal insights that will stay with you long after you've reached Santiago.

Chapter 13: Camino Reflections and Life Lessons

The Camino de Santiago is a journey that touches the soul as much as it tests the body. For many, the memories and insights gained along the way linger long after they've returned home. Walking hundreds of kilometers, meeting fellow travelers, and being immersed in the simplicity of the Camino has a way of awakening reflections and sparking life lessons. In this chapter, we'll dive into stories and insights from past pilgrims, explore the profound personal growth that many experience, and look at ways to carry the Camino spirit forward even after the journey has ended.

Stories and Insights from Past Pilgrims

Every pilgrim who has walked the Camino carries a unique story, each one shaped by individual backgrounds, motivations, and experiences. Listening to these stories reveals the Camino's profound ability to connect people from different walks of life and provides inspiration for those about to embark on their own journey.

María's Journey of Healing: María, a 45-year-old woman from Argentina, began her Camino as a way to process grief after losing her father. She recalls that each step became a form of therapy, especially when she found herself walking through the peaceful forests on the Camino Primitivo. "I didn't realize how much I was holding inside until I was alone on the trail. The Camino gave me space to let go of that sadness," she shared. By the time María reached Santiago, she felt a sense of peace she hadn't thought possible and came away with the insight that sometimes healing doesn't need answers—just space and time.

Peter's Transformation from Businessman to Pilgrim: Peter, a retired businessman from the UK, saw the Camino as a physical challenge. Yet, somewhere between the Meseta's endless plains and the camaraderie of shared albergue meals, he found himself questioning his previous definition of success. "I thought I needed achievements to be fulfilled," he reflected, "but on the Camino, nobody cared about my past accomplishments. It was freeing to be seen as just another pilgrim." Peter's journey taught him the value of simplicity and humility, lessons he now incorporates by volunteering and giving back to his community.

Ling's Discovery of Self-Worth: Ling, a young woman from Singapore, walked the Camino Francés after feeling directionless in her career and personal life. She initially set out to "find herself," though the journey taught her something different. "What I found was strength I didn't know I had," she explained. When she faced blisters, exhaustion, and self-doubt, Ling realized that the path to self-worth wasn't in changing her life but in learning resilience. Today, she sees each challenge as an opportunity to reinforce the strength she discovered on the Camino.

These stories underscore the Camino's power to reveal parts of ourselves we may not recognize in daily life. Every pilgrim encounters moments of joy, frustration, peace, and sometimes even frustration, but these emotions form the rich tapestry of a journey that is unlike any other.

Personal Growth Through the Journey

Walking the Camino is often a journey of transformation, not because of a set destination, but because of the daily practice of letting go, trusting the path, and confronting one's own limitations. Many pilgrims discover new layers of resilience, kindness, patience, and self-compassion along the way.

Building Resilience: The Camino tests physical and mental endurance. Blisters, sore muscles, and long hours of walking push pilgrims to their limits. Yet, every pilgrim learns that resilience grows not from avoiding discomfort but from moving through it. Each difficult day adds to a pilgrim's sense of inner strength, which often surprises them. Many pilgrims who doubted their physical ability at the start find themselves reaching Santiago, feeling more resilient than ever before.

Developing Patience: In our fast-paced world, patience can be a rare virtue. But on the Camino, everything slows down. Some pilgrims may take longer to reach a destination than they expect, have to wait for a shower, or find themselves waiting in line at an albergue. These small moments teach patience, showing that the journey itself has its own timing. Pilgrims often carry this patience back to daily life, approaching situations with a newfound calm.

Practicing Self-Compassion: Many people are used to pushing themselves to do more, be more, or achieve more. The Camino teaches a different lesson—that self-compassion is vital to a meaningful journey. There will be days when a pilgrim feels exhausted or discouraged. The Camino invites them to accept these feelings, rest, and start fresh the next day. This practice of self-compassion is often one of the most valuable gifts a pilgrim brings home, reminding them to be gentle with themselves even when life feels challenging.

Each lesson learned on the Camino contributes to personal growth that extends far beyond the journey itself. Whether it's resilience, patience, or self-compassion, these qualities shape pilgrims long after they leave the trail, becoming part of their everyday lives.

Finding Meaning and Purpose on the Camino

Many pilgrims set out on the Camino in search of deeper meaning or a sense of purpose. The journey offers a unique opportunity to strip away the distractions of daily life and reflect on what truly matters. For some, this experience confirms the direction they're already on, while for others, it's a turning point.

Discovering Simplicity: Living out of a backpack for weeks teaches pilgrims how little they actually need to feel content. This simplicity often brings a sense of peace, helping many pilgrims realize that happiness isn't tied to material things. For many, the Camino becomes a lesson in valuing experiences over possessions, relationships over status, and self-awareness over external validation.

Connecting with Others: The Camino is a melting pot of people from different cultures, ages, and backgrounds, and yet, on the trail, everyone is united as pilgrims. Many find that these connections provide a sense of meaning and community. It's not uncommon to share deep conversations with strangers who may become lifelong friends. The bonds created on the Camino remind pilgrims of the value of genuine connections and the power of shared experiences.

Renewing Spirituality: For some, the Camino is a spiritual pilgrimage, and walking it serves as a way to renew their faith or find peace with questions about life and existence. The presence of churches, crosses, and sacred sites along the way offers a chance to reflect, pray, and seek guidance. Even for those who are not religious, the Camino can be a deeply spiritual experience, providing a space for introspection, gratitude, and reverence.

Many pilgrims find that the Camino becomes a symbol of the values they want to carry forward. Some return home with a clearer sense of purpose, while others find new meaning in relationships, careers, or personal goals. The Camino often illuminates a path toward a more fulfilling life.

Staying Connected to the Camino Spirit After Returning

One of the greatest challenges pilgrims face is holding onto the Camino's lessons after returning to daily life. The sense of freedom, simplicity, and connection that permeates the Camino can sometimes feel distant once the journey ends. However, many pilgrims find creative ways to keep the Camino spirit alive in their everyday lives.

Practicing Gratitude: On the Camino, pilgrims often feel grateful for simple things—a good meal, a comfortable bed, or a kind gesture from a fellow walker. After returning, some pilgrims make it a daily habit to practice gratitude, finding that it helps them appreciate life's small joys. Writing in a gratitude journal or simply taking a moment each day to acknowledge blessings can help preserve the spirit of the Camino.

Reconnecting with Nature: The Camino immerses pilgrims in beautiful landscapes, and many find peace in nature along the way. After returning home, some pilgrims continue to spend time in nature, whether through local hikes, daily walks, or camping trips. Staying connected to nature allows them to revisit the calm and clarity they experienced on the trail.

Staying Involved in the Camino Community: Many pilgrims join Camino associations, attend pilgrim reunions, or participate in online forums to stay connected with others who have walked the Way. Being part of this community offers support, camaraderie, and a reminder of the shared experiences that unite all who have walked the Camino.

Volunteering at Albergues or Camino-Related Events: Some pilgrims return to volunteer as hospitaleros (volunteer albergue hosts) to give back to the

Camino. Hosting new pilgrims offers a chance to relive the journey from a different perspective, providing encouragement and comfort to others. This form of service helps them stay engaged with the Camino's spirit while supporting future pilgrims.

Incorporating Camino Values into Daily Life: The Camino teaches lessons of kindness, simplicity, resilience, and mindfulness. Many pilgrims strive to carry these values into their everyday lives by embracing slower living, prioritizing meaningful relationships, and approaching challenges with patience and self-compassion.

Returning from the Camino doesn't mean leaving its lessons behind. By making conscious choices, pilgrims can keep the spirit of the Camino close, finding ways to infuse their lives with the meaning, peace, and purpose they discovered on the trail.

In Camino Reflections and Life Lessons, we see how the Camino's impact reaches far beyond the physical journey. Pilgrims carry home not just a Compostela but a wealth of memories, insights, and lessons that continue to shape their lives. Each story, each moment of personal growth, each connection made, and each life lesson learned on the Camino becomes part of a pilgrim's journey—a journey that doesn't end in Santiago but continues as they walk through the paths of daily life, forever changed by the Way.

Stories and Insights from Past Pilgrims: The Depth of Connection

Pilgrims often describe their Camino journey as an experience that creates a profound connection—not only with themselves but with the world around them. Each story shared along the Camino becomes part of a larger tapestry that gives the Camino its unique character. Whether it's finding peace in solitude or discovering camaraderie with strangers, every pilgrim's insight adds a new dimension to the journey. Here are more stories that reflect the Camino's lasting impact:

Elena's Path to Forgiveness: Elena, a woman in her 50s from Italy, came to the Camino carrying a heavy burden of unresolved conflicts with family members. She had tried therapy, self-help books, and long conversations, but nothing seemed to ease the resentment. However, on the Camino, she found that forgiveness came more naturally. "Walking every day in silence gave me a chance to let go of my anger. I realized that forgiveness wasn't about the other person; it was about finding peace in my own heart." Elena's story is a powerful reminder that sometimes, physical movement can help release emotional pain.

Tomás and His Rediscovery of Joy: Tomás, a retiree from Spain, had been struggling with depression and found it difficult to find joy in daily life. He embarked on the Camino hoping to lift his spirits, though he was initially skeptical. "One day, I found myself dancing with a group of other pilgrims at a small albergue," he said with a laugh. "I hadn't danced in years, but in that moment, I felt alive again." Tomás's story reflects how the Camino, with its spontaneity and human connection, can awaken joy even in those who have forgotten what it feels like.

Yuki's Lesson in Vulnerability: Yuki, a young woman from Japan, was used to handling everything on her own. But an injury on the Camino forced her to lean on others. "Asking for help was the hardest thing I'd ever done," she shared. "But in doing so, I learned that there's strength in vulnerability." Yuki's experience shows that the Camino can teach powerful lessons about community, interdependence, and the courage it takes to open up to others.

These stories reveal the wide range of insights and emotions that the Camino uncovers. Whether it's forgiveness, joy, or vulnerability, each journey is a unique process of self-discovery. The Camino has a way of pulling us out of our comfort zones and challenging the stories we tell ourselves about who we are and what we're capable of.

Personal Growth Through the Journey: The Path as a Teacher

Walking the Camino provides lessons that no classroom or book can teach. With every hill climbed, every meal shared, and every morning sunrise, the Camino teaches its pilgrims valuable lessons that shape how they see themselves and the world. Here are some deeper ways in which the Camino fosters personal growth:

Acceptance of Uncertainty: On the Camino, there's no telling what each day will bring. The weather might change, an albergue might be full, or a detour might be necessary. The Camino trains pilgrims to accept the unknown with grace. Many find that this lesson sticks with them, helping them face life's unpredictability with a calmer, more adaptable mindset.

Cultivating Presence: In everyday life, people often rush from one task to another, rarely stopping to enjoy the moment. On the Camino, the only goal each day is to walk, eat, and rest. This slower pace teaches pilgrims to appreciate the present and find beauty in the small details—a warm cup of coffee, the crunch of gravel underfoot, or the colors of a sunset. This ability to live in the moment often becomes a lasting gift, helping pilgrims find calm and contentment even after they return home.

Embracing Simplicity: Carrying only the essentials on your back for weeks teaches a valuable lesson in simplicity. Pilgrims quickly learn what's truly necessary and how little they actually need to feel happy. This realization often translates into a more minimalist lifestyle back home, with many pilgrims adopting practices that prioritize experiences and relationships over material possessions.

The Camino, with its simplicity and rhythm, is a powerful teacher. Every challenge it presents offers an opportunity to grow, and every step taken is a reminder that personal growth is less about achieving perfection and more about embracing the journey.

Finding Meaning and Purpose on the Camino: The Quest for Understanding

Many pilgrims come to the Camino during times of transition or when searching for a deeper sense of purpose. On the trail, without the distractions of daily life, many find that clarity and purpose emerge naturally. Here are some ways that pilgrims find new meaning on the Camino:

Rediscovering Values: For some, the Camino becomes a place to reassess what truly matters. Away from work, technology, and daily routines, many pilgrims rediscover the values that bring them joy and fulfillment. Some decide to make life changes based on these insights, whether it's spending more time with family, dedicating themselves to a cause, or pursuing a career aligned with their passions.

Reevaluating Success: In a world that often measures success by achievements, status, or wealth, the Camino offers a refreshing contrast. Many pilgrims come to see success as something much simpler—feeling fulfilled, helping others, or simply enjoying the present moment. For those who leave corporate jobs or busy lifestyles, the Camino provides a chance to redefine what success looks like on their own terms.

Seeking Inner Peace: The Camino's quiet beauty and steady pace offer a refuge for those seeking inner peace. Many find that simply walking day after day allows them to release worries, regrets, and anxieties that they've been carrying. By the time they reach Santiago, many pilgrims feel lighter, not just physically, but emotionally, having found a sense of peace that comes from letting go.

For those who walk the Camino with an open heart and mind, the journey often reveals a new sense of meaning and purpose. These insights become guiding stars that continue to light their path even after they leave the Camino.

Staying Connected to the Camino Spirit After Returning: Bringing the Journey Home

Returning home after the Camino can be both joyful and challenging. Many pilgrims miss the simplicity and connection they felt on the trail and look for ways to carry that spirit into their everyday lives. Here are more ways to stay connected to the Camino long after the journey ends:

Creating Rituals: Many pilgrims establish daily or weekly rituals that remind them of the Camino. This could be a quiet morning walk, a time to journal, or lighting a candle for gratitude. These rituals keep the Camino's values alive, reminding pilgrims of the insights they gained and helping them stay centered.

Finding Local Pilgrim Communities: Pilgrims often find comfort and camaraderie by connecting with others who have walked the Camino. Many cities have local Camino groups or associations that organize meetups, lectures, or hikes. Being part of this community allows pilgrims to continue sharing stories, reliving memories, and supporting one another.

Volunteering and Giving Back: The Camino relies on volunteers to keep its network of albergues, churches, and facilities running. Many former pilgrims feel called to give back by volunteering as hospitaleros (albergue hosts) or by joining Camino associations. Serving other pilgrims offers a meaningful way to stay connected, while giving back to the path that gave them so much.

Embracing Pilgrim Values in Relationships: The Camino is known for its atmosphere of kindness, generosity, and openness. Many pilgrims choose to carry these values into their personal relationships, making an effort to be more compassionate, listen more deeply, and show kindness in everyday interactions. These small acts help keep the Camino spirit alive and foster stronger connections with family, friends, and even strangers.

Journaling and Reflecting Regularly: Some pilgrims find it helpful to set aside time each month to reflect on their Camino experience. Whether it's reading through old journal entries, looking through photos, or simply recalling memories, this practice helps them stay connected to the lessons they learned. It also offers an opportunity to see how far they've come since their journey, and to realign with the values they discovered on the path.

The Camino de Santiago is more than a physical journey; it's a path that winds through the soul, leaving pilgrims forever changed. Whether it's in the stories of past pilgrims, the lessons learned along the way, the meaning discovered, or the ways to stay connected, the Camino offers gifts that last a lifetime. Each step, each experience, and each lesson becomes a part of who you are, guiding you long after you've returned home.

By carrying the Camino spirit with you, you become part of a timeless tradition, one that encourages you to approach life with openness, gratitude, resilience, and kindness. And so, even after you leave the physical path behind, the Camino's journey continues—through every action, every choice, and every moment of connection. In this way, the Camino never truly ends; it becomes a part of you, shaping how you walk through life, one step at a time.

Chapter 14: Preparing for the Unexpected

Walking the Camino de Santiago is an unforgettable journey, but it also comes with its share of surprises. Even the best-laid plans can face disruptions along the way, whether from unpredictable weather, difficult terrain, or cultural differences. Being prepared for these situations can make your pilgrimage smoother and more enjoyable. This chapter dives deep into practical strategies for handling unexpected challenges on the Camino, from dealing with language barriers to staying safe in bad weather.

Handling Bad Weather and Terrain Changes

Weather on the Camino can be unpredictable. In a single day, you might start with clear skies, face rain by midday, and find yourself in gusty winds by afternoon. The changing landscapes along the Camino routes—from coastal paths to mountain passes—bring their own weather challenges. Here's how to be ready for any type of weather or terrain the Camino might throw your way.

Preparing for Rain

Rain is common on the Camino, especially if you're walking in spring or fall. Wet weather can make trails slippery and affect visibility. A few key items can help you manage rainy days:

Waterproof Gear: A good-quality rain jacket or poncho is essential. Look for something that covers both you and your backpack. Waterproof covers for your backpack keep your belongings dry, and gaiters can be useful in protecting your lower legs and feet from mud.

Footwear: Invest in waterproof hiking boots with good traction. Wet trails, especially on rocky or muddy terrain, can be hazardous. Proper footwear keeps you steady and reduces the risk of blisters.

Ziploc Bags: These are great for storing electronics, maps, or any items that need to stay dry.

Dealing with Wind

Wind can be particularly challenging on high ridges and exposed areas along the Camino. Strong gusts make walking harder, especially if you're carrying a full backpack.

Layering: Layers provide warmth and flexibility. Choose wind-resistant clothing and make sure your top layer is both windproof and breathable.

Securing Loose Items: Make sure everything is secured to your backpack. Gusts can blow away items like hats or gloves, so use carabiners or secure pockets.

Managing Cold Weather

If you're walking in the early spring or late fall, or if you're on a higher-altitude route, temperatures can drop significantly. Mornings and evenings may be chilly, and you'll want to stay warm without overheating as you walk.

Layering for Warmth: Start with a moisture-wicking base layer, add a warm mid-layer (such as fleece), and finish with a windproof outer layer. Wearing a hat, gloves, and scarf helps keep your extremities warm.

Hot Drinks: Many cafes and albergues serve hot beverages. Take advantage of these stops to warm up and keep your body temperature stable.

Handling Hot Weather

The Camino can be scorching in the summer months, especially in regions like the Meseta on the Camino Francés. Walking in the heat requires extra precautions to stay safe and hydrated.

Start Early: Walking in the early morning hours helps you avoid the hottest part of the day. Aim to finish your walking by early afternoon.

Hydrate Regularly: Drink water frequently and carry a water bottle or hydration bladder. Refill whenever you have the chance, and consider adding electrolyte tablets if you're sweating heavily.

Sun Protection: Use a wide-brimmed hat, sunglasses, and sunscreen. Covering exposed skin with lightweight, breathable clothing also provides protection.

The weather can change quickly on the Camino, and being prepared for a variety of conditions will help you stay comfortable and safe.

What to Do If You Get Lost

Getting lost on the Camino isn't uncommon, especially if you're on a lesser-traveled route or miss a waymark. Fortunately, most routes are well-marked, but it's still possible to take a wrong turn. Here's what to do if you find yourself off the path.

Watch for Yellow Arrows and Markers

The Camino is famously marked with yellow arrows, often painted on trees, rocks, or buildings. If you go for a while without seeing an arrow, it's a sign you may have missed a turn.

Retrace Your Steps: When you realize you're off-route, retrace your steps to the last marker you saw. Often, going back a short distance can help you find the correct path.

Ask for Help: Don't hesitate to ask locals for directions. Basic Spanish phrases like "¿Dónde está el Camino?" (Where is the Camino?) can be very helpful. Many locals are familiar with the route and are happy to assist.

Use Navigation Apps

While many pilgrims prefer the traditional experience of following the arrows, having a GPS app can be reassuring if you get lost. Some apps work offline, so you don't need data service.

Wise Pilgrim and Buen Camino Apps: These apps are designed specifically for Camino routes and have maps, stage information, and accommodations listed. Download maps before your trip, so they're accessible offline.

Google Maps Offline: You can download an offline map of your route area on Google Maps. This can help you navigate back to a familiar point if you stray too far.

Stay Calm and Assess

If you're completely lost, stay calm. Take a break, drink some water, and evaluate your surroundings. Look for familiar landmarks, or use your guidebook's maps to get a sense of dircction. Getting lost can feel stressful, but it's often just a small detour.

Tips for Traveling During Holidays and Festivals

Spain is known for its lively festivals, and many towns along the Camino have their own unique celebrations. While these can make your journey more colorful, they also mean crowded accommodations, altered schedules, and sometimes limited services.

Plan Ahead for Major Holidays

Some holidays, like Semana Santa (Holy Week) and Día de Santiago (St. James's Day), bring an influx of tourists and pilgrims. This can make finding accommodations challenging.

Book Accommodations in Advance: If you know you'll be walking through a town during a major holiday, consider booking a bed ahead of time. Popular towns can fill up quickly, and having a reservation saves you from a stressful end to your day.

Arrive Early: If you're not able to book ahead, plan to arrive at your destination town earlier than usual. This gives you a better chance of securing a bed at an albergue before it fills up.

Enjoy the Festivities

While holidays can mean more crowds, they also provide a chance to witness Spain's vibrant culture firsthand. Many towns have processions, concerts, and feasts during these times.

Participate in Local Events: Join in the festivities if you can. Experiencing a local festival adds a special dimension to your journey. Ask locals about events, and they'll often be excited to share the best places to watch or participate.

Prepare for Limited Services: During major holidays, many shops and services may be closed. Plan ahead by stocking up on essentials like water, snacks, and other supplies the day before a holiday.

Spain's festivals are a memorable part of the Camino experience, so embrace the energy and festivities as part of your pilgrimage.

Dealing with Language Barriers

While many locals along the Camino are used to pilgrims and may know some English, it's helpful to have a few basic Spanish phrases at your disposal. Simple phrases and polite gestures can go a long way in easing communication.

Learn Key Spanish Phrases

Knowing even a few Spanish words shows respect and helps bridge the gap. Common phrases like "por favor" (please), "gracias" (thank you), and "¿Cuánto cuesta?" (How much does it cost?) are very useful.

Useful Phrases for Pilgrims:

"¿Dónde está el albergue?" (Where is the hostel?)

"¿Tiene cama libre?" (Do you have a free bed?)

"¿A qué hora cierran?" (What time do you close?)

"Una cerveza y una tapa, por favor" (One beer and a snack, please)

Use Translation Apps

There are several language apps that can help you in a pinch. Google Translate, for example, can translate text, voice, and even images. Download Spanish for offline use, as Wi-Fi might not always be available.

Be Patient and Smile

When language fails, patience and friendliness go a long way. Smiling, nodding, and making eye contact show that you're respectful and trying to communicate. Spaniards are generally welcoming and patient with pilgrims, and a little effort is often appreciated.

Non-Verbal Communication

If you're struggling, try using gestures and pointing. Many situations can be handled with a bit of charades, whether it's ordering food, asking for directions, or understanding instructions at an albergue.

Language barriers might feel intimidating at first, but they're often an opportunity to connect with locals and fellow pilgrims in new and memorable ways.

Flexible Planning for Last-Minute Changes

Flexibility is one of the most valuable traits a pilgrim can have. The Camino is unpredictable—accommodations may be full, weather may turn, or you may simply decide to change your pace. Being open to adjustments allows you to embrace the Camino experience without unnecessary stress.

Be Open to Daily Adjustments

Your original plan may look very different once you're on the trail, and that's okay. Some days you'll feel strong and ready to cover more ground, while others you may want a shorter, slower day.

Consider Shorter or Longer Stages: If you're exhausted, cut your day short and stay in a smaller town. Conversely, if you have extra energy and the conditions are good, you can continue to the next village or town. Flexibility in daily distance lets you listen to your body and adapt to how you feel in the moment.

Have a Few "Plan B" Options

Knowing a few nearby towns or villages along your route provides alternatives if your original destination isn't possible. Carrying a guidebook or using a Camino app can help you see other nearby stops.

Nearby Villages: Familiarize yourself with the nearby locations so you have options if you encounter a full albergue or want a quieter night. Many small villages along the Camino have lesser-known albergues that aren't as crowded.

Backup Accommodations: Some areas may have hotels or guesthouses if albergues are full. Although they're often more expensive, knowing where these options are located can be a lifesaver if your day doesn't go as planned.

Make Use of Rest Days

Including rest days or shorter walking days in your plan can be refreshing. Whether it's a break in a larger city like Burgos or León or just an extra morning in a quiet village, rest days help you recharge both physically and mentally.

Allow for Recovery: Rest days help prevent injuries, particularly blisters, knee pain, or sore muscles. Giving your body time to recover can improve the quality of your entire pilgrimage.

Explore Local Culture: Use rest days to explore the history, culture, and cuisine of the places you're visiting. Larger towns along the Camino often have museums, cathedrals, and local markets worth experiencing.

Embrace the Unexpected

One of the joys of the Camino is its unpredictability. You might meet someone who invites you to a local event, or find a scenic spot where you want to linger longer. Embracing these moments and allowing your plan to change will open doors to experiences you didn't anticipate.

Say "Yes" to Surprises: Be open to spontaneous decisions, like joining a group for a meal or taking a scenic detour. These moments often become the highlights of the Camino.

Stay Positive: Unexpected changes can be stressful, but they're also part of the adventure. Keep a positive mindset and remind yourself that flexibility is part of the journey. Accepting the unknown and staying adaptable often leads to meaningful experiences.

In Summary

Preparing for the unexpected on the Camino means being ready for weather challenges, language barriers, crowded accommodations, and changes to your daily routine. By staying flexible, keeping an open mind, and carrying a few essential tools (both literal and mental), you'll be able to handle the Camino's surprises with ease. Every twist and turn, whether planned or unplanned, adds to the richness of your pilgrimage. As you face these moments with resilience and adaptability, you'll discover that each unexpected experience is a unique chapter in your Camino journey.

Embrace Flexibility as Part of the Camino Experience

One of the most beautiful aspects of the Camino is that it encourages flexibility and a willingness to let go of rigid plans. Pilgrims often start with specific itineraries, but the Camino has a way of reshaping even the best-laid plans. Whether due to weather, physical limitations, or simply the urge to stay longer in a certain place, many find that embracing flexibility becomes one of the most valuable parts of the experience.

Letting Go of Daily Expectations

Each day on the Camino brings new challenges and surprises. Some days you'll cover more ground than expected, while other days might be cut short by unexpected fatigue or a hidden gem of a village that invites you to stay. The ability to let go of daily expectations and listen to your body, your instincts, and even the people you meet along the way allows for a richer, more fulfilling pilgrimage.

Building Resilience Through Adaptability

The Camino teaches resilience by showing you how to adapt to the unexpected. You may start your journey with specific expectations about what you'll accomplish each day, but the Camino's twists and turns remind you to stay open and adaptable. Each adjustment strengthens your resilience, teaching you to face challenges with a calm and open mind. From adapting to the weather to changing plans based on energy levels or unexpected encounters, resilience becomes a muscle that grows stronger with each day's walk.

Handling Accommodation Shortages and Crowded Albergues

The Camino can become quite busy during peak seasons, especially in spring and fall. On popular routes like the Camino Francés, albergues often fill up quickly, especially in smaller towns or during festival periods. Learning how to handle accommodation shortages will give you peace of mind and help you stay flexible in your planning.

Early Starts for Better Availability

Starting early in the morning is a common strategy for pilgrims who want to secure beds in albergues. By setting out before dawn, you give yourself a head start on finding accommodation by early afternoon. Early starts are particularly helpful on days when you plan to stop in smaller towns with limited beds.

Checking Availability Along the Way: Many pilgrims call ahead or ask other walkers for information on bed availability. Some albergues allow reservations, especially in busier towns, so it's worth checking if you have a preferred stop in mind.

Alternative Accommodation Options

If your chosen albergue is full, there are still other options. Many towns along the Camino offer a variety of accommodations beyond traditional pilgrim hostels, from private albergues to guesthouses and small hotels. While these might be pricier than albergues, they're often less crowded and offer additional comforts.

Pensions and Hostales: These small guesthouses provide simple rooms for pilgrims and are available in most towns along the Camino. Although they don't have the communal feel of albergues, they offer privacy and sometimes include breakfast.

Local Hotels and Casas Rurales: For a break from the albergue experience, local hotels or rural homes (casas rurales) provide a comfortable option. They're especially useful if you want a restful night or a bit more space.

Stay Calm and Look for Nearby Alternatives

If you find yourself without a bed in your planned town, don't panic. Most towns on the Camino have alternative options, and many locals are willing to direct you to nearby accommodations. Flexibility and calmness go a long way, and sometimes these unexpected stays can lead to memorable experiences, as smaller albergues and guesthouses often have a unique charm.

Managing Limited Services on the Camino

One of the unique aspects of the Camino is that it winds through rural areas, where shops and services may be limited, particularly in smaller villages. Knowing how to manage limited resources is an important part of preparing for the unexpected.

Carrying Basic Supplies

In remote stretches or small towns, you may find fewer places to buy supplies. It's wise to carry a small stock of essentials, like snacks, water, and basic first aid supplies, especially if you're walking through rural areas or if it's a Sunday when many shops are closed.

Food and Snacks: Granola bars, nuts, dried fruit, and chocolate are easy to carry and provide quick energy. Keep these on hand, especially for long stretches between towns or on days with limited services.

First Aid Essentials: A small first-aid kit with blister treatments, bandages, and pain relievers can be a lifesaver in remote areas. Even minor issues like blisters can become serious if untreated, so having supplies is essential.

Know the Service Schedule

It's helpful to be aware of when services are available in smaller towns, especially in rural Spain where shops often close for siesta in the afternoon and many businesses are closed on Sundays. Planning around these schedules will ensure you're not caught without essential supplies.

Siesta Closures: Many businesses close between 2 PM and 5 PM, so plan to purchase food or other items outside these hours. Larger cities may have more continuous service, but in rural towns, it's common for shops and cafes to close for several hours.

Sunday Closures: In Spain, Sunday is traditionally a day of rest, and many businesses, including grocery stores, are closed. Plan to stock up on essentials the day before, so you have everything you need.

Adjusting to Fewer Amenities

Some albergues, especially the more rustic municipal ones, may lack amenities like hot water, private showers, or Wi-Fi. Embracing these simpler accommodations as part of the Camino experience helps foster gratitude for the essentials and makes the more comfortable stops feel like a luxury.

Embracing Unpredictability as Part of the Journey

One of the greatest lessons the Camino can teach is the value of embracing unpredictability. While it's natural to want everything to go smoothly, the unexpected moments often bring the most meaningful insights and memories. Whether it's a change in plans, a chance encounter, or a detour, seeing these moments as opportunities rather than obstacles enriches your Camino experience.

Finding Joy in Spontaneity

The Camino is a living, breathing path with a personality of its own. It's often said that "the Camino provides," meaning that the journey seems to offer exactly what each pilgrim needs, whether that's a moment of reflection, a new friendship, or even a challenging day that teaches resilience.

Trusting the Process: Trust that each step on the Camino has value, even if it doesn't align with your original plan. The detours and surprises are often where the Camino's magic lies.

Connecting with Fellow Pilgrims: Some of the best memories are made when plans change, and you find yourself sharing a meal, a story, or a moment of laughter with fellow pilgrims who are also navigating the unexpected.

Seeing Challenges as Part of the Adventure

Unexpected challenges are a part of any pilgrimage, and the Camino is no different. Instead of seeing these as setbacks, approach them as opportunities to grow, learn, and embrace the unpredictable nature of life.

Every Challenge is a Lesson: Each unexpected situation brings a chance to learn something new, whether about yourself, your fellow pilgrims, or the Camino itself. From small inconveniences to more significant challenges, these moments often hold valuable lessons in patience, resilience, and compassion.

Building a Story Worth Telling: The unexpected is what makes every Camino unique. When you look back on your pilgrimage, it's likely these moments—the ones that required you to adapt, persevere, and trust—that will stand out the most.

In Preparing for the Unexpected, you've gathered strategies and insights that will serve you well on the Camino. Embracing flexibility, staying open to changes, and remaining adaptable are all part of what makes the Camino experience so transformative. Each unexpected event, from changing weather to last-minute detours, is a chance to grow and deepen your connection to the pilgrimage. With these tools in hand, you'll be ready to face anything that comes your way, turning every challenge into a meaningful part of your journey.

Chapter 15: Useful Phrases and Local Language Tips

The Camino de Santiago weaves through beautiful landscapes and charming villages, but one of the most rewarding parts of the journey is the people you meet along the way. Whether you're chatting with locals in a small cafe, asking for directions, or simply sharing stories with fellow pilgrims, language plays a huge role in creating connections. While many locals and other pilgrims understand basic English, having some knowledge of Spanish phrases and Camino-specific terminology will make your experience smoother and more meaningful. Here's a guide to essential phrases, Camino-specific vocabulary, communication tips, and helpful translation apps that will ease your interactions along the way.

Basic Spanish Phrases for the Camino

Learning a few basic Spanish phrases can make a big difference on the Camino, even if you're only visiting Spain for a short time. These common phrases will help you navigate everyday interactions, from ordering food to finding directions and understanding local customs. Here's a handy list of must-know phrases:

Greetings and Politeness:

Hola – Hello
Buenos días – Good morning
Buenas tardes – Good afternoon
Buenas noches – Good evening / Good night
Adiós – Goodbye
Hasta luego – See you later
Por favor – Please
Gracias – Thank you
De nada – You're welcome
Perdón / Disculpe – Excuse me / I'm sorry

Basic Questions:

¿Dónde está…? – Where is…?

¿Cuánto cuesta? – How much does it cost?

¿Tiene una cama libre? – Do you have a bed availabl¿A qué hora abren / cierran? – What time do you open/close?

¿Puedo usar el baño? – Can I use the bathroom?

¿Hay un cajero automático cerca? – Is there an ATM nearby?

Navigational Phrases:

A la derecha – To the right

A la izquierda – To the left

Recto / Todo recto – Straight ahead

Cerca / Lejos – Near / Far

Estoy perdido/a – I'm lost

¿Dónde está el Camino? – Where is the Camino?

¿Cuánto falta hasta…? – How far is it to…?

Ordering Food and Drink:

Un café, por favor – A coffee, please

Una botella de agua, por favor – A bottle of water, please

¿Tiene menú del día? – Do you have a daily menu?

Una cerveza / vino, por favor – A beer / wine, please

Sin gluten / Vegetariano – Gluten-free / Vegetarian

La cuenta, por favor – The bill, please

¿Se puede pagar con tarjeta? – Can I pay with a card?

Health and Emergencies:

Me duele… – I have pain in…

Necesito ayuda – I need help

Llama a una ambulancia – Call an ambulance

¿Dónde está el hospital? – Where is the hospital?

Tengo alergia a… – I'm allergic to…

While you may not need all of these phrases every day, knowing the basics will make communication easier and show locals that you respect their language and culture.

Knowing even a little Spanish can transform your experience on the Camino. In addition to helping you with practical things like ordering food or asking for directions, speaking Spanish can bridge the gap between you and the locals who live along the Camino. It's a sign of respect and can lead to richer, more memorable interactions.

Additional Practical Phrases:

¿Está abierto/abierta? – Is it open?

¿A qué hora sale…? – What time does (it) leave? (For buses, trains, etc.)

¿Dónde puedo encontrar…? – Where can I find…?

Estoy buscando… – I am looking for…

¿Cuánto tiempo falta para llegar a…? – How long until we reach…?

¿Podría ayudarme? – Could you help me?

¿Puedo sentarme aquí? – Can I sit here?

Expressing Needs and Feelings:

Tengo hambre – I am hungry.

Tengo sed – I am thirsty.

Estoy cansado/cansada – I am tired (masculine/feminine).

Necesito descansar – I need to resEstoy perdido/perdida – I am lost (masculine/feminine).

Necesito agua – I need water.

Me duele la pierna/el pie – My leg/foot hurts.

For Shopping and Supplies:

¿Dónde puedo comprar...? – Where can I buy...?

¿Cuánto cuesta este? – How much does this cost?

Es demasiado caro – It's too expensive.

¿Tienen uno más barato? – Do you have a cheaper one?

¿Tienen crema para ampollas? – Do you have blister cream?

These phrases cover a range of everyday situations and can help you navigate albergues, cafes, and local stores. Locals are often more than willing to help if they see you're making an effort with the language.

Food and Drink Essentials:

Food and drink are big parts of the Camino experience. Many towns and villages along the way have traditional dishes and local specialties worth trying. Knowing how to order and ask questions about food will help you make the most of it.

¿Qué recomienda? – What do you recommend?

¿Qué hay para comer? – What is there to eat?

Sin carne, por favor – Without meat, please (helpful for vegetarians).

¿Tiene algo sin gluten? – Do you have something gluten-free?

Otra ronda, por favor – Another round, please (if you're with friends and want another drink).

Una mesa para uno/dos/tres, por favor – A table for one/two/three, please.

Getting Accommodation:

Finding a place to sleep is essential after a long day on the Camino. The following phrases will help you secure a spot at an albergue, hotel, or hostel.

¿Hay camas disponibles? – Are there beds available?

¿Cuánto cuesta por noche? – How much per night?

¿Está incluido el desayuno? – Is breakfast included?

¿A qué hora es la salida? – What time is checkout?

Necesito una habitación privada, por favor – I need a private room, please.

¿Dónde puedo dejar mi mochila? – Where can I leave my backpack?

These phrases will help you secure accommodation and understand what each place offers. Many albergues operate on a first-come, first-served basis, so knowing these terms can speed up the check-in process.

For Personal Needs and Emergencies:

After days of walking, you may need supplies for self-care, medical assistance, or even a break. Here's how to communicate those needs.

¿Dónde está la farmacia? – Where is the pharmacy?

¿Tienen algo para las ampollas? – Do you have something for blisters?

Me siento enfermo/enferma – I feel sick (masculine/feminine).

¿Hay algún lugar para descansar? – Is there a place to rest?

Necesito algo de hielo – I need some

¡¿Dónde puedo conseguir agua? – Where can I get water?

Mastering these essential phrases can give you more confidence and independence on the Camino, allowing you to navigate all aspects of daily life smoothly.

Camino Terminology

The Camino has its own language, full of words and phrases unique to the pilgrimage experience. Understanding these terms will help you navigate your journey more smoothly and feel part of the Camino community. Here are some of the most common words you'll encounter:

Albergue – A hostel specifically for pilgrims, offering budget-friendly, often shared accommodations.

Credencial del Peregrino – The pilgrim passport, which you use to collect stamps at each stop. This serves as proof of your pilgrimage and is required to earn your Compostela in Santiago.

Compostela – The official certificate awarded in Santiago to pilgrims who complete at least 100 kilometers on foot or 200 kilometers by bike or horseback.

Etapa – A stage or segment of the Camino, often referring to a daily walking distance.

Peregrino/Peregrina – Pilgrim (masculine/feminine), the term used to describe all walkers on the Camino.

Botafumeiro – The large incense burner swung in Santiago Cathedral during special pilgrim masses.

Hospitalero/Hospitalera – Volunteer or staff member who manages an albergue. They often provide information, guidance, and support to pilgrims.

Sellos – Stamps collected along the route in your Credencial as proof of your journey.

Jacobeo – Related to St. James, patron saint of the Camino. You may see this term used to describe holy years (Año Jacobeo) or festivities in honor of St. James.

Misa del Peregrino – The pilgrim mass, typically held in churches along the route, offering blessings to pilgrims.

Mochila – Backpack; a term you'll hear frequently, as pilgrims often ask each other about what they're carrying. Knowing these words will help you feel more integrated into the pilgrimage experience and make it easier to follow directions, ask for help, and understand signs along the way.

The Camino has a vocabulary all its own, filled with unique words and phrases that reflect its long-standing traditions and culture. Understanding these terms will help you feel more comfortable in conversations with other pilgrims and locals.

More Camino-Specific Words and Phrases:

Jacobeo/Año Jacobeo – The Holy Year of St. James, celebrated when July 25 (St. James Day) falls on a Sunday. During these years, the Camino sees an increase in pilgrims, and additional services and blessings are offered.

Refugio – A shelter or refuge along the route, sometimes similar to an albergue but typically simpler or more rustic. Some refugios operate on a donation basis, reflecting the Camino's spirit of generosity.

Mojón – Stone marker or post often bearing the yellow arrow symbol that guides pilgrims along the path. You'll find these markers frequently along the route.

Camino Francés – The most popular route of the Camino, starting from Saint-Jean-Pied-de-Port in France and covering about 780 kilometers to Santiago.

Camino Portugués, Camino del Norte, Camino Primitivo, Via de la Plata – Other well-known Camino routes. Each route has its own character, scenery, and unique challenges, offering pilgrims a choice based on their preferences and fitness.

Montón de piedras – Pile of stones; some pilgrims place stones along the Camino as a symbol of letting go of burdens, often on hilltops or near specific markers.

Ultreia – A Latin term meaning "Onward!" that pilgrims use to encourage one another. It's common to hear it along the Camino as a word of motivation.

These terms are part of what makes the Camino feel like a distinct, shared experience. Embracing the unique language of the Camino can help you feel like part of a community that stretches back centuries.

The Camino has evolved its own vocabulary, with terms that convey the culture, spirit, and practical aspects of the pilgrimage. Here are some more unique and frequently used terms:

Pilgrim Rituals and Terms:

Concha de Vieira – The scallop shell, the universal symbol of the Camino. Many pilgrims wear a scallop shell on their backpack, symbolizing their journey and connection to all who've walked the Camino before them.

Cruz de Ferro – The Iron Cross, located near Foncebadón on the Camino Francés. Here, pilgrims often leave a stone brought from home, symbolizing the release of burdens.

Río y fuente – River and fountain; you'll encounter many along the Camino. Some are legendary for their healing waters, like the Fonte do Carme in Galicia.

Bienvenidos Peregrinos – "Welcome, pilgrims!" A phrase often seen at albergues and in towns along the route.

Pilgrimage Tools and Essentials:

Bordón – The traditional pilgrim's walking staff, often adorned with a cross or other symbol.

Polvo – Dust; refers to the dirt that coats everything after hours on unpaved trails. You'll hear "¡Cuidado con el polvo!" (Watch out for the dust!) in areas with heavy foot traffic.

Lavandería – Laundry facilities. Some albergues offer lavandería services or have machines for washing and drying clothes.

Knowing this vocabulary will make the Camino experience feel more intimate, giving you a stronger sense of tradition and understanding of the pilgrimage culture.

Tips for Communicating with Locals

The Camino runs through many small villages and rural areas where locals may speak little or no English. Engaging with locals can be one of the most enriching aspects of the Camino, offering insight into Spanish culture and connecting you to the region's traditions. Here are some tips for smoother communication with locals:

Start with a Greeting: Always greet people with "hola" or "buenos días" before launching into a question. Spaniards appreciate politeness, and a simple greeting shows respect and friendliness.

Speak Slowly and Clearly: Even if you don't speak much Spanish, speaking slowly and using simple words can make a big difference. Avoid slang and keep sentences straightforward.

Use Hand Gestures: Gestures can bridge the gap when words fail. Pointing, nodding, or miming actions can help you convey your meaning, and many locals are used to using body language with pilgrims.

Carry a Small Notebook: Writing things down can be helpful, especially when dealing with numbers, addresses, or specific instructions. For example, if you're asking for directions or inquiring about bus times, jotting down key words or phrases can prevent misunderstandings.

Learn Key Local Phrases: Besides Spanish, you may encounter regional dialects like Galician or Basque, depending on your route. Learning a few basic words in the local dialect can endear you to locals and make your interactions more memorable.

Practice Patience: Communication may take a bit more time, especially in smaller villages. Be patient and stay relaxed—locals often appreciate your effort to connect, even if there's a language barrier.

Building rapport with locals can add depth to your Camino experience. Locals often have rich stories to share and a deep knowledge of the area, so embracing these connections can make your journey even more meaningful.

The Camino is an international pilgrimage, but it passes through rural Spain, where English may not be widely spoken. Being able to communicate, even with basic Spanish, will make your journey much easier and more enjoyable. Here are some additional tips and cultural insights to keep in mind:

Use a Friendly Tone and Body Language:

A smile and friendly tone can go a long way, especially in smaller towns where locals may not be used to English-speaking visitors. A positive attitude shows you're approachable, making locals more likely to help you.

Remember Siesta Hours:

Spain has a tradition of siesta, a midday break where many shops and businesses close, especially in rural areas. Siesta times usually last from around 2 PM to 5 PM. Be mindful of this when planning your stops and interactions with locals. Asking "¿Está abierto?" (Is it open?) before entering a shop during these hours can save you some frustration.

Learn the Politeness Norms:

Politeness is highly valued in Spanish culture. Using "por favor" (please), "gracias" (thank you), and "disculpe" (excuse me) shows respect and appreciation. For example, when asking for directions, start with a polite "disculpe" and end with "gracias."

Engage with Local Culture:

If you stay in smaller villages, show interest in local traditions, foods, or customs. Asking about local dishes ("¿Qué recomienda de comer aquí?" – What do you recommend to eat here?) or expressing curiosity about the area can lead to wonderful exchanges and insights.

Practice Basic Numbers:

Numbers are essential when asking about prices, distances, or times. Here's a quick guide:

Uno, dos, tres… – One, two, three…

Diez – Ten

Veinte – Twenty

Treinta – Thirty

Cuarenta – Forty

Cincuenta – Fifty

Cien – One hundred

Be Aware of Regional Dialects:

While Spanish is the main language along the Camino, you'll also pass through regions with distinct dialects, like Galician in Galicia. Locals may use Galician phrases in their daily speech, but they'll switch to Spanish if you address them in it.

By making an effort with these tips, you're likely to create positive interactions that add depth and warmth to your Camino experience.

Understanding the nuances of Spanish culture can make interactions smoother and help you feel more at ease in rural Spain. Here's a deeper dive into effective communication tips for connecting with locals:

Understand the Importance of Timing:

Spanish daily life often runs on a different schedule than what many visitors are used to. Lunch happens later, usually around 2 PM, and dinner is typically after 8 PM. If you're looking for a meal or trying to visit a shop, be mindful that many places close during siesta hours and may not reopen until later in the afternoon.

Try Spanish Greetings and Farewells with Fellow Pilgrims:

Using simple Spanish greetings with other pilgrims can add a sense of camaraderie. A friendly "¡Buen Camino!" (Good way/journey!) is a common greeting exchanged between pilgrims, symbolizing encouragement and goodwill. When departing, "¡Hasta luego!" (See you later!) or "¡Que te vaya bien!" (Wishing you well!) adds warmth to your interactions.

Be Mindful of Personal Space and Eye Contact:

In Spain, maintaining eye contact while speaking is considered polite, showing respect and attentiveness. Personal space, however, can vary— Spaniards may stand closer in conversations than is typical in some cultures, especially in rural areas. Don't feel uncomfortable if people stand closer while chatting; it's a sign of engagement and friendliness.

Show Interest in Local Culture:

People in smaller towns often take pride in their local traditions, and showing curiosity can create a deeper bond. Try asking about local food specialties, festivities, or legends tied to the Camino. Simple questions like "¿Cuál es la comida típica de aquí?" (What's the typical food here?) or "¿Hay alguna historia interesante sobre este pueblo?" (Is there an interesting story about this town?) are conversation starters that can lead to memorable interactions.

Express Gratitude for Their Hospitality:

Thanking locals for their hospitality, especially in smaller albergues or family-owned cafes, goes a long way. "Muchas gracias por todo" (Thank you for everything) or "Ha sido muy amable" (You have been very kind) are ways to express your appreciation.

Tips for Communicating with Other Pilgrims from Different Countries:

The Camino brings people from all over the world, so you may hear many languages. Being open to other languages and customs can be just as valuable as learning Spanish. If you find yourself with non-English-speaking pilgrims, a shared effort to communicate creates bonds regardless of language differences.

By following these tips, you're likely to experience the warmth and kindness of Spanish hospitality and create memories that go beyond just the walking itself.

Handy Translation Apps for Travelers

Even with basic Spanish phrases and Camino terminology, there may be times when you need a bit more help with translation. Smartphone apps can be lifesavers when navigating language challenges. Here are some of the best translation apps for the Camino:

Google Translate: Google Translate is one of the most popular options, offering text, voice, and photo translation. You can download the Spanish language pack for offline use, which is helpful when Wi-Fi is unavailable. The app's camera translation feature is especially handy for translating signs or menus instantly.

iTranslate: This app offers voice and text translation, and a paid version includes offline capabilities. It's easy to use, with a clean interface, making it ideal for quick, on-the-go translations.

SpanishDict: While not a full translation app, SpanishDict is fantastic for learning phrases, basic grammar, and vocabulary. It's particularly helpful if you want to learn a bit more Spanish as you go, and it includes example sentences for real-world context.

Reverso: Reverso is another reliable app that's especially good for idiomatic expressions. The app provides translation context, which is useful for understanding colloquial Spanish phrases that may not translate directly.

SayHi Translate: This app specializes in voice-to-voice translation, so you can simply speak into the app, and it will translate your words into Spanish (and vice versa). It's great for conversational situations where typing is inconvenient.

Using a translation app as a backup can make your interactions smoother and give you confidence in situations where language barriers feel overwhelming. Just remember to keep your phone charged, as translation apps can drain battery quickly.

Incorporating language learning and local phrases into your Camino experience will deepen your connection with the journey. From simple greetings to essential terminology, knowing the basics of Spanish and Camino lingo will make the path feel more welcoming and accessible. And while translation apps can be incredibly helpful, nothing beats a smile, a warm greeting, and a few kind words in the local language. Engaging with locals and fellow pilgrims, even in simple ways, will add to the richness of your Camino experience, creating memories and connections that last long after you've returned home.

Having a translation app on your phone can be a lifesaver for quick translations, especially in moments where basic phrases might not be enough. Here's a deeper look at the best apps to consider, along with tips for making the most of them:

Google Translate:

This app is incredibly versatile and offers:

Text Translation: Type in phrases or sentences for instant translation.

Voice Translation: Speak into the app, and it will translate your words. This is especially helpful in conversations.

Image Translation: Use the camera to translate text in real-time, perfect for reading signs, menus, or informational plaques.

Offline Use: Download the Spanish language pack for offline access, which is useful in remote areas with limited internet.

iTranslate:

This app has a clean interface and is beginner-friendly, with a focus on simplicity. Its offline mode (available in the premium version) lets you translate common phrases and essential words, even without data. It also offers a conversation mode, where both users can speak into the app for quick back-and-forth translations.

SpanishDict:

For those who want to learn more Spanish along the way, SpanishDict is ideal. It provides contextual translations, grammar tips, and common phrases, making it more than just a translation tool. You can use it to deepen your Spanish knowledge and build vocabulary that will make future interactions easier.

Reverso:

Known for its accuracy with idiomatic expressions, Reverso helps clarify meanings for phrases that may not translate directly. This is useful for more complex conversations or when interacting with locals who may use casual, everyday language that's harder to understand.

SayHi Translate:

This voice-focused app is user-friendly, allowing you to speak directly into the app and hear the translation in real time. SayHi is ideal for quick interactions, especially if you're on the go and can't type or read text translations.

Tips for Using Translation Apps on the Camino:

Conserve Battery: Translation apps can quickly drain your phone's battery. Use them sparingly, or carry a portable charger.

Practice Key Phrases: Apps are helpful in the moment, but taking time each day to practice commonly used phrases will reduce your dependence on technology.

Use the Camera Feature for Menus: Spanish menus often list regional foods or special preparations. Using the camera feature can help you understand unfamiliar dishes and make ordering easier.

Translation apps are valuable tools, but try not to rely on them exclusively. A few practiced words, combined with gestures and a friendly attitude, often lead to more memorable and meaningful interactions.

Translation apps can be incredibly useful, but maximizing their potential requires a few extra tricks. Here's a more detailed guide on how to use them effectively on the Camino:

Using Google Translate's Camera Feature for Cultural Context:

In some towns, you'll find historical plaques, signs about local legends, or even signs for regional foods. Using Google Translate's camera feature helps you understand these details, making the experience richer. Point the camera at a plaque or menu, and the app will overlay translations, helping you learn more about the places you're passing through.

Offline Language Packs as a Safety Net:

Even though the Camino routes pass through many towns, there are stretches without consistent phone reception. Downloading the Spanish language pack in advance will let you use the app without internet, ensuring that you have access to essential translations at all times.

Using Apps for Pronunciation:

If you're unsure about pronouncing a phrase, some apps like iTranslate or SpanishDict allow you to listen to native pronunciations. Practicing key phrases, especially those related to greetings or directions, can give you confidence when speaking with locals.

Setting Up Pre-Saved Phrases for Quick Use:

Many apps allow you to save common phrases, so consider creating a list of frequently used expressions for easy access. Examples include "¿Dónde está el baño?" (Where is the bathroom?) and "¿Tiene un menú del peregrino?" (Do you have a pilgrim menu?). Having these saved will make it quicker to pull them up when you need them.

Respectful Usage of Apps During Conversations:

While translation apps are handy, pulling out your phone mid-conversation can sometimes seem impolite. Use them as a backup rather than as a primary tool. Try to attempt the phrase first, then turn to the app if you're stuck. Locals will appreciate your effort to speak their language, even if it's not perfect.

Connecting Translation Apps with Cultural Resources:

Some translation apps can connect with cultural resources, showing additional context for phrases or idioms. For example, you might look up "Buen Camino" and find explanations about the cultural significance of the phrase. This added layer of meaning can deepen your appreciation for Camino traditions.

Final Thoughts on Language and Connection

Language is an essential tool on the Camino, not only for practical navigation but for connecting with the rich culture of Spain and the community of fellow pilgrims. Every interaction—whether it's ordering a meal, chatting with a fellow pilgrim, or asking a local for directions—becomes an opportunity to immerse yourself more deeply in the experience.

Don't worry about getting everything right; the Camino is a place where effort is valued over perfection. Every attempt to communicate, whether it's through a few basic phrases, hand gestures, or a translation app, brings you closer to the spirit of the Camino. Pilgrims and locals alike appreciate when travelers make an effort to connect through language, even if it's just a simple greeting or "gracias." These small exchanges are part of what makes the Camino so special, fostering a shared understanding that transcends words.

The Camino is a journey where kindness, humility, and openness mean more than fluency. Each "¡Buen Camino!" you hear is a reminder that everyone on this path shares a common purpose, and every interaction, no matter how brief or challenging, enriches that experience. So as you prepare for your journey, consider this chapter as more than just a list of words and tips. It's a toolkit for connection—helping you bridge differences, open doors to new friendships, and experience the warmth of Camino culture firsthand.

Whether it's through Spanish, gestures, a smile, or simply the act of walking together, the Camino creates a unique language of its own, one that welcomes everyone who takes the path. Embrace it, and let every word, every greeting, and every interaction deepen your understanding and appreciation of the Camino de Santiago.

Useful Phrases and Local Language Tips, is more than a list of vocabulary; it's a bridge that connects you to the people, places, and culture of the Camino. By learning some essential phrases, understanding Camino-specific terminology, and following these communication tips, you'll find it easier to engage with locals and fellow pilgrims. Communication is a powerful tool for creating deeper connections and memories on your journey, and even small efforts to speak the language will be appreciated and reciprocated with warmth and hospitality.

Chapter 16: Essential Camino de Santiago Resources

Preparing for the Camino de Santiago involves more than just packing the right gear and planning a route. There's a wealth of resources that can help you make the most of your journey, from books and documentaries that provide insight and inspiration to mobile apps and support groups that keep you connected and informed on the trail. This chapter covers essential resources to guide your journey, providing the tools you need to navigate, plan, and connect with the Camino community.

Recommended Books and Documentaries

Books and documentaries on the Camino de Santiago offer valuable perspectives, both practical and inspirational. Whether you're looking for detailed maps, historical background, personal memoirs, or spiritual reflections, these resources can deepen your understanding and connection to the pilgrimage.

Books

A Pilgrim's Guide to the Camino de Santiago by John Brierley
One of the most popular guidebooks, this resource covers the Camino Francés with detailed maps, spiritual insights, and practical advice. Brierley's guidebook is particularly beloved for its section-by-section breakdowns, which include daily stages, points of interest, and historical context. It's a perfect companion for pilgrims seeking both logistical help and a deeper spiritual connection to the path.

The Way of the Pilgrim by Anonymous
Originally a Russian Orthodox text, this book is not specific to the Camino but provides insight into the universal themes of pilgrimage, contemplation, and faith. Many Camino walkers find it helpful for understanding the mental and spiritual aspects of a journey that goes beyond physical boundaries.

The Pilgrimage by Paulo Coelho
This novel recounts Coelho's own journey along the Camino and introduces themes of self-discovery,

transformation, and resilience. Blending fiction with autobiography, Coelho's work inspires readers to reflect on the internal journey of the Camino and find deeper meaning in each step.

Off the Road: A Modern-Day Walk Down the Pilgrim's Route into Spain by Jack Hitt

In this humorous memoir, Jack Hitt shares his personal experiences on the Camino, blending historical insights with lighthearted observations. His writing provides a balanced view, offering both the beauty and the unexpected challenges that make the Camino a unique experience.

Walking Home: A Pilgrimage from Humbled to Healed by Sonia Choquette

Choquette's memoir is about healing and self-discovery. After experiencing several personal losses, she embarks on the Camino to find inner peace. Her journey speaks to the emotional healing that the Camino can offer, making it relatable for those walking through a time of change or loss.

To the Field of Stars: A Pilgrim's Journey to Santiago de Compostela by Kevin A. Codd

Codd, a Catholic priest, offers a reflective and deeply spiritual account of his pilgrimage. His story dives into the highs and lows of the journey, balancing humor and vulnerability with profound reflections on faith, community, and the transformative power of the Camino.

Documentaries

Walking the Camino: Six Ways to Santiago

This documentary follows six pilgrims from diverse backgrounds as they navigate the Camino Francés. Each pilgrim's journey reveals a different aspect of the Camino, from the physical challenges to the emotional rewards. It's an inspiring film that captures the personal growth, camaraderie, and resilience that define the Camino.

The Way

Directed by Emilio Estevez and starring Martin Sheen, this fictional story follows a father walking the Camino after his son's death. While not a documentary, it captures the emotional journey of the Camino, focusing on themes of family, healing, and self-discovery. The film has inspired many to walk the Camino and is widely appreciated by pilgrims for its respectful portrayal of the journey.

Footprints: The Path of Your Life

This documentary follows a group of young men from Arizona as they tackle the Camino with a focus on spirituality and brotherhood. Their journey highlights the physical and spiritual challenges of the pilgrimage, illustrating how the Camino fosters personal and collective growth.

Camino Skies

A powerful and emotional film that follows six pilgrims from New Zealand and Australia, each walking the Camino in the wake of personal tragedy. The documentary emphasizes the healing aspect of the Camino, offering insight into how the journey helps pilgrims process grief and rebuild their lives.

I'll Push You

This touching documentary tells the story of two lifelong friends, one of whom is confined to a wheelchair. Together, they embark on the Camino, with one friend pushing the other for over 800 kilometers. It's a testament to friendship, determination, and the power of the Camino to bring people closer together.

These books and documentaries bring the Camino to life, offering you a chance to learn, reflect, and prepare for your own pilgrimage.

Camino Websites and Forums for Planning

Online resources have transformed the way pilgrims prepare for the Camino, providing access to a wealth of advice, route information, and personal stories. Here are some of the best websites and forums to help you plan and connect with others.

Camino de Santiago Forum (camino-de-santiago-forum.com)

This forum is a top resource for Camino walkers, with discussions on every aspect of the journey. Topics cover routes, packing, safety, albergues, and personal experiences, offering a supportive community where you can ask questions, get recommendations, and read up on other pilgrims' insights. Many seasoned Camino walkers share tips that only come from firsthand experience, making this forum invaluable for both beginners and return pilgrims.

Gronze.com

Primarily in Spanish, Gronze is one of the most comprehensive websites for planning the Camino. It offers detailed route descriptions, updated albergue information, and cost estimates. Each Camino route has its own section, including photos and interactive maps. If you're looking for reliable, up-to-date information on where to stay and how to budget, Gronze is an excellent choice.

American Pilgrims on the Camino (americanpilgrims.org)

For North American pilgrims, this organization provides support, events, and resources, including local chapters that host Camino talks and meetups. The website includes links to route maps, packing lists, and Camino basics, along with information on obtaining your Credencial.

Camino Ways (caminoways.com)

Camino Ways is a travel company that specializes in organized Camino tours, but their website is packed with free information, including packing lists, training tips, and articles about Camino traditions and history. While the focus is on promoting tours, it's a useful resource for general Camino knowledge.

Eroski Consumer Camino de Santiago (caminodesantiago.consumer.es)
This Spanish site offers detailed information on every stage of the Camino, with maps, photos, albergue details, and even weather forecasts. The site is particularly helpful for those following the Camino Francés but also covers lesser-known routes.

Camino Ninja
Camino Ninja is a popular app-based platform offering albergue information, route maps, and GPS-based tracking. The website complements the app, providing articles and insights about route options, health and safety tips, and resources for planning.

These websites and forums offer a well-rounded base for planning, giving you a sense of the logistics, costs, and community awaiting you on the Camino.

Top Mobile Apps for Navigation and Booking

While the Camino is well-marked with signs and arrows, having a mobile app can enhance your journey by providing real-time guidance, accommodation options, and helpful reminders. Here are some of the best Camino apps:

Wise Pilgrim
This app covers nearly all the main Camino routes, providing route maps, albergue listings, and daily stage recommendations. The offline maps feature is particularly useful, allowing you to navigate even in areas without

mobile coverage. Wise Pilgrim is a favorite among pilgrims who prefer a digital guidebook without the weight of a printed book.

Buen Camino App (Eroski Consumer)

Developed by Eroski Consumer, this app offers detailed maps, route information, and albergue listings with user reviews. The app also provides estimated distances and times for each stage, making it easy to plan your day-to-day walk. Buen Camino's interface is straightforward and user-friendly.

Booking.com

While not Camino-specific, Booking.com can be very helpful for booking accommodations in larger towns along the route. The app allows you to reserve hotels, hostels, and guesthouses, which can be reassuring during busy periods or if you need a break from the albergue experience.

Camino Pilgrim

Camino Pilgrim offers maps, route details, and practical information on accommodations and amenities along various Camino routes. It's designed for flexibility, allowing you to adjust stages according to your pace and energy. Camino Pilgrim is especially helpful if you prefer to customize your route.

Camino Ninja

Camino Ninja focuses on providing albergue information with real-time availability updates, route maps, and tracking. The app also offers a social feature, allowing you to see other pilgrims on the same route, which adds a sense of community and security.

Google Maps and Maps.me

While not specific to the Camino, both Google Maps and Maps.me can be useful for general navigation, especially in towns and cities. Maps.me allows offline map downloads, which is ideal for remote areas. Google Maps is helpful for locating specific addresses, shops, or cafes along the way.

These apps bring the Camino to your fingertips, ensuring you have access to navigation, accommodations, and real-time updates to make your journey smoother.

Camino Associations and Support Groups

Camino associations and support groups offer a wealth of resources and a sense of community, both online and in person. Many of these groups provide local events, pre-departure advice, and connections with other pilgrims. Being part of a Camino association can also open up opportunities for volunteering, whether by supporting Camino infrastructure or hosting Camino-related events.

The Confraternity of Saint James (CSJ)

Based in the United Kingdom, the Confraternity of Saint James is one of the oldest Camino associations outside Spain. They offer extensive resources, from guidebooks to practical advice on health and safety. The CSJ also publishes a series of detailed guides for various Camino routes and has a library of Camino literature. For UK pilgrims, the CSJ organizes talks, workshops, and social gatherings that help connect Camino enthusiasts at all stages of their journey.

American Pilgrims on the Camino (APOC)

APOC is the leading Camino organization in the United States, with a mission to support pilgrims before, during, and after their journey. APOC has regional chapters across the U.S., and members frequently host Camino training hikes, information sessions, and events to prepare new pilgrims. The group also provides the Credencial for American pilgrims, and the APOC website has a wealth of articles, recommended reading, and packing tips.

Canadian Company of Pilgrims

This Canadian group offers a strong support network for Canadian pilgrims. They provide resources like packing lists, route planning advice, and even organized training walks. The Canadian Company of Pilgrims also facilitates the distribution of Credenciales and organizes events that foster a strong Camino community in Canada.

Society of Saint James (Sociedad de San Jaime)

Located in Spain, the Sociedad de San Jaime offers resources in Spanish, supporting Spanish-speaking pilgrims or those comfortable with the language. This group maintains connections with various Camino albergues and provides logistical information for all major routes.

Australian Friends of the Camino

This organization provides support for Australian pilgrims, offering access to Camino resources and hosting events across Australia. Members can attend Camino talks, receive practical advice on long-distance walking, and connect with other Australians who have walked or are planning to walk the Camino.

Pilgrim Support Groups on Social Media

Facebook has numerous Camino-specific groups where you can connect with a global community of current and former pilgrims. Groups like "Camino de Santiago (The Way of St. James)" or "Camino de Santiago Pilgrims" provide forums where you can ask questions, share experiences, and find encouragement. These groups are helpful for real-time support and advice.

Joining an association or support group can enhance your Camino experience, providing resources and a sense of camaraderie. Whether you're preparing for your first Camino or reliving memories from past journeys, these groups connect you with like-minded people who understand the unique beauty and challenges of the pilgrimage.

Contacts and Emergency Information for Pilgrims

While the Camino is generally safe and welcoming, having emergency contact information can provide peace of mind. Here are essential contacts and resources you should have on hand:

Emergency Services

In Spain, the national emergency number is 112. This connects you to police, medical, and fire services. Spanish emergency responders are trained to handle cases involving international visitors, so you can expect a helpful response if you need assistance.

Pilgrim Assistance Points

Certain towns along the Camino have pilgrim assistance centers, often connected to albergues, churches, or tourism offices. These centers offer help to pilgrims dealing with injuries, lost items, or logistical issues. Ask at any albergue for information on the nearest assistance point.

Hospitals Along the Camino Francés

While there are many hospitals along the Camino, here are a few located in major towns that are accustomed to assisting pilgrims:

Hospital de San Pedro in Logroño

Hospital Universitario de Burgos in Burgos

Hospital Universitario de León in León

Complejo Hospitalario de Navarra in Pamplona

Hospital Clínico Universitario in Santiago de Compostela

These hospitals can handle a range of medical issues, from minor injuries to more serious concerns. Pilgrims can walk into most of these facilities without an appointment, although some smaller clinics may require a wait.

Embassy and Consulate Contacts

If you're from outside the EU, it's useful to have your country's embassy or consulate contact information in case of legal, medical, or logistical issues. Here are some of the main embassies in Madrid:

United States Embassy: +34 915 87 22 00

United Kingdom Embassy: +34 917 14 63 00

Canadian Embassy: +34 914 233 250

Australian Embassy: +34 91 353 6600

Having these numbers saved on your phone is wise, especially if you need assistance with lost passports, visas, or legal matters.

Camino Helpline Services

Several Camino support organizations offer helplines for pilgrims in need. These numbers vary depending on your route, but you can usually find information at albergues or from other pilgrims. If you're in doubt, a local albergue manager can often help guide you to the right resources.

Tourist Information Centers

Many towns along the Camino have tourist information centers where you can get maps, ask about local amenities, or find emergency contacts. Tourist offices are typically located in the town center, near plazas or cathedrals, and offer helpful advice on nearby services.

Having this emergency contact information on hand gives you an extra layer of security, ensuring that help is never far away if you encounter an issue along the Camino.

This chapter on resources gives you the practical tools you'll need to navigate every aspect of the Camino. From books and documentaries that prepare you mentally and emotionally, to support groups and emergency contacts that keep you safe and connected, these resources are here to guide you through every step. Whether you're looking for community, spiritual insights, logistical tips, or real-time support, these resources enrich the Camino experience, helping you feel prepared and confident as you embark on one of the most meaningful journeys of your life.

In preparing for the Camino de Santiago, this collection of resources becomes your personal toolkit for a successful and enriching journey. From the early stages of planning to the moment you set foot on the trail, these books, apps, forums, and contacts keep you connected to a wealth of information and support.

Recommended Reading and Documentaries provide inspiration and deeper insights, bringing the Camino's history, spirituality, and challenges into sharper focus. Whether you're looking to explore the lives of past pilgrims or learn from the real-life experiences of others, these materials help you understand what the Camino has meant to those who walked it before you.

Camino Websites and Forums are your best companions for planning, offering firsthand advice from experienced pilgrims and insights on everything from what to pack to what to expect on each stage of the journey. Engaging with online Camino communities introduces you to fellow walkers, giving you a sense of the Camino's extensive and supportive network.

Mobile Apps have changed the way pilgrims experience the Camino, bringing route maps, accommodation options, and local information right to your pocket. Whether you're reserving an albergue or tracking your route, these apps allow you to navigate the Camino with confidence and ease.

Associations and Support Groups connect you to a global network of Camino enthusiasts and offer practical help, encouragement, and a chance to give back. By joining a local or international Camino organization, you gain access to invaluable resources, events, and friendships that enrich your journey and help maintain the Camino's legacy.

Emergency Contacts and Assistance Points are vital for peace of mind. Knowing that help is only a phone call away, whether for medical assistance, lost items, or directions, allows you to walk with greater confidence. Keeping these contacts handy ensures that you're prepared for any situation, allowing you to focus on the beauty of the journey and the meaningful experiences that await.

As you set out on the Camino de Santiago, remember that you're not alone—these resources provide a bridge to the broader Camino community. Each of these tools helps you navigate the path ahead, but they also connect you to a journey that extends far beyond the trail. In the true spirit of the Camino, every resource, connection, and piece of advice serves as a reminder that the Camino is as much about the people and experiences along the way as it is about reaching Santiago. This collection of resources enriches your journey, ensuring you're prepared, connected, and supported every step of the way.

The Camino de Santiago isn't just a physical journey; it's a deeply personal experience that touches the mind, body, and spirit. By tapping into the resources here, you're setting yourself up for a journey that's not only safe and well-prepared but also profoundly enriched by the insights, stories, and community around you. These resources aren't just tools—they're gateways into the rich legacy, traditions, and spirit of the Camino.

Imagine opening John Brierley's guidebook on your first day, understanding each landmark and village with new depth, or reading Kevin Codd's reflections in To the Field of Stars, resonating with the same highs and lows you'll encounter along the path. Documentaries like Walking the Camino give you a taste of the camaraderie, the struggles, and the inner transformations that await, bringing you into the lives of those who have journeyed before you. The books and films you explore before setting foot on the Camino help create a roadmap, not only of the physical terrain but also of the emotions and experiences you might face.

Then there are the online communities and forums that bring the Camino to life even before you leave home. Connecting with other pilgrims on platforms like the Camino de Santiago Forum can be a revelation; you'll find veterans who've walked multiple routes and are eager to share tips, recommendations, and encouragement. By joining the conversation early, you're building a support network that doesn't end when you reach Santiago—it's a lifelong community. Some pilgrims find friends on these forums with whom they later meet up on the trail, creating bonds that stretch across countries and continents.

When you're on the Camino, mobile apps become invaluable for making real-time decisions. Imagine reaching a small town after a long day's walk and pulling out the Wise Pilgrim app to find the nearest albergue, complete with reviews from other pilgrims. Or, perhaps you're in need of a good meal; with Camino Ninja, you'll get recommendations for nearby cafes and restaurants that welcome weary walkers. And if you ever find yourself uncertain of the path, a quick glance at your offline map from Maps.me can help you get back on track without worry. These apps provide peace of mind, giving you the freedom to focus on the journey rather than logistics.

As you connect with Camino associations and support groups, you're not just preparing for a single trip; you're becoming part of a centuries-old tradition of pilgrimage that countless people around the world hold dear. Associations like the Confraternity of Saint James or American Pilgrims on the Camino offer invaluable resources that support every stage of your pilgrimage. From training walks that prepare you physically, to events that connect you with seasoned pilgrims, these groups offer community and guidance that last far beyond your time on the trail. Many pilgrims find themselves returning to these associations as volunteers, giving back to the Camino community and helping to preserve the path for future walkers.

And in the unlikely event that you encounter an emergency, having contacts and assistance points readily available is a reassuring safeguard. Knowing you can call for help at any time—whether it's reaching local authorities via Spain's 112 emergency number, finding a nearby hospital accustomed to aiding pilgrims, or contacting your country's embassy for support—gives you the confidence to tackle challenges head-on. The Camino is safe, but life can bring unexpected situations, and being prepared allows you to walk with peace of mind.

Together, these resources transform the Camino from a physical path into a journey deeply rooted in knowledge, preparation, and community. They remind you that the Camino isn't just about reaching Santiago—it's about every connection, insight, and experience along the way. As you walk, you carry the wisdom of past pilgrims, the support of fellow walkers, and the guidance of those who've dedicated themselves to preserving this remarkable path.

Each resource you turn to is like a companion on your journey, guiding and supporting you through the highs and lows. With this foundation, you're stepping onto the Camino not just as a traveler but as a pilgrim ready to embrace all that the journey has to offer. In the end, these tools aren't just about reaching a destination; they're about deepening the journey itself, helping you uncover the Camino's hidden gems, both within the landscape and within yourself.

Chapter 17: Frequently Asked Questions about the Camino

Walking the Camino de Santiago is an adventure filled with excitement, but it also brings up questions for both first-time and returning pilgrims. From concerns about safety to practical travel tips, here's an in-depth look at some of the most commonly asked questions. These answers will help you prepare for the journey with confidence, so you can focus on making memories rather than worrying about logistics.

Is the Camino Safe for Solo Travelers?

Safety is a top priority for many pilgrims, especially those planning to walk the Camino alone. The Camino is widely regarded as one of the safest long-distance hikes in the world, and solo travel is extremely common on this route. Here's why it's a safe option for solo travelers and some tips to ensure you feel secure throughout your journey:

A Well-Established Route: The Camino has been a pilgrimage path for centuries, with clear waymarks, dedicated pilgrim accommodations, and towns spaced out for convenient rest stops. Because of this, you're rarely isolated, even in the quieter sections of the route.

Supportive Pilgrim Community: One of the most unique aspects of the Camino is the strong sense of community among pilgrims. You'll often meet others walking at a similar pace, and it's common to form friendships along the way. Many solo travelers find companionship with others, creating informal "Camino families" that help each other throughout the journey.

Help is Readily Available: The Camino's popularity means that local residents, albergue staff, and fellow pilgrims are familiar with the needs of walkers. If you ever feel lost or in need of help, you're likely just a short distance away from assistance, whether it's a nearby pilgrim, a friendly local, or a designated help center.

Tips for Solo Travelers:

Trust Your Instincts: Like any travel experience, trust your intuition. If something doesn't feel right, change your plans or ask for help.

Stick to Popular Routes: The Camino Francés, for example, is heavily traveled, making it an excellent choice for solo walkers due to the presence of other pilgrims and frequent accommodations.

Keep Friends or Family Informed: Share your daily plans with someone back home. Many pilgrims keep in touch through social media, emails, or texts, providing an added layer of safety.

The Camino is designed for all types of travelers, and solo pilgrims are embraced as part of the Camino's diverse community. Walking alone can be deeply empowering, offering a chance for self-reflection and independence in a supportive environment.

What's the Best Way to Get to the Starting Point?

Choosing your starting point on the Camino is an important decision, as each route and location offers a different experience. Here are some of the main starting points and how to get there from major international hubs:

Saint-Jean-Pied-de-Port (Camino Francés): This is one of the most popular starting points for the Camino Francés, located in France near the Spanish border.

From Paris: You can take a train from Paris to Bayonne, then transfer to a smaller train that goes directly to Saint-Jean-Pied-de-Port. Alternatively, some pilgrims fly into Biarritz and then take a train or bus.

From Madrid or Barcelona: Direct trains and buses from these cities to Pamplona, then onward to Saint-Jean-Pied-de-Port via a local shuttle or private transport.

Lisbon or Porto (Camino Portugués): The Portuguese Way is typically started in either Lisbon or Porto, with

Porto being the more common starting point.

From Lisbon: Fly into Lisbon and begin your walk from there, or take a train or bus to Porto to start from there.

From Madrid or Barcelona: Direct flights to Porto are available, or you can take an overnight train or bus.

Oviedo (Camino Primitivo): For pilgrims interested in the Camino Primitivo, Oviedo is the main starting point.

From Madrid: There are direct flights from Madrid to Oviedo, or you can take a train or bus.

From Santiago de Compostela: If you've already been to Santiago and want to walk back, buses and trains connect Santiago with Oviedo.

Irun (Camino del Norte): This coastal route often starts in Irun, near the border between Spain and France.

From Madrid or Barcelona: There are direct trains to San Sebastián, which is close to Irun. From there, you can take a local train or bus to Irun.

Additional Tips:

Use Pilgrim Shuttle Services: Many companies offer pilgrim shuttle services from major cities to popular starting points, which can simplify your travel arrangements.

Consider a Starting Point in Spain: If you're flying internationally, consider starting your Camino at a major city within Spain itself (such as León or Pamplona). This option can save travel time and may be easier for first-time pilgrims.

Plan for a Rest Day: Arriving at your starting point a day before you start walking gives you time to adjust, gather supplies, and rest after your travels.

Choosing the right starting point is the first step of your Camino journey. With so many well-connected cities and transportation options, reaching your starting point can be as smooth and convenient as possible.

Do I Need Travel Insurance?

Travel insurance is highly recommended for anyone walking the Camino. Even if you're in good health and experienced in long-distance travel, unexpected situations can arise, from medical emergencies to travel delays. Here's what to look for when choosing travel insurance for the Camino:

Medical Coverage: Look for a policy that includes medical expenses, as healthcare costs can add up, especially in case of an emergency. Your insurance should ideally cover doctor visits, hospitalization, and any necessary medications. This is particularly important for international travelers who are not covered by Spain's public healthcare system.

Evacuation Coverage: Some routes, especially the Camino Primitivo and Camino del Norte, pass through mountainous or remote areas. Having evacuation coverage is beneficial if you encounter a serious injury and need specialized transport to a hospital.

Trip Cancellation or Delay: Delays are common in travel, especially if your journey involves multiple connections. Coverage for trip cancellation or delay can help cover unexpected accommodation or transportation costs if your plans change.

Lost or Stolen Baggage: While theft on the Camino is rare, it's not unheard of. Coverage for lost or stolen belongings, including your backpack, can save you the hassle of replacing gear and essentials.

How to Choose a Policy:

Look for Pilgrim-Specific Insurance: Some insurance providers offer policies tailored to pilgrims, covering the unique risks associated with walking the Camino.

Check Your Existing Coverage: Some credit cards or health insurance plans may provide limited coverage abroad. Confirm what's covered and supplement with travel insurance if necessary.

Carry a Copy of Your Policy: Keep a physical or digital copy of your insurance policy with you, including the emergency contact numbers.

Insurance is a small investment that brings peace of mind, allowing you to walk the Camino knowing you're prepared for unexpected situations.

How Much Does the Camino Cost Overall?

One of the most appealing aspects of the Camino is that it can fit a wide range of budgets. While it's possible to walk the Camino on a shoestring budget, other pilgrims prefer a more comfortable experience. Here's a breakdown of typical costs on the Camino:

Accommodation: Albergues (pilgrim hostels) are the most affordable option, typically costing €5-€15 per night for a bed in a dormitory. Private rooms in albergues or budget hotels range from €25-€40 per night, while mid-range hotels or private accommodations can be €50-€100 or more per night.

Food: Pilgrim menus are available in most restaurants along the Camino, costing around €10-€15 for a three-course meal, including wine. Breakfast and lunch can be simpler, with costs around €3-€5 for coffee and a pastry, or €5-€10 for a sandwich or snack.

Transportation: If you're flying internationally, flights will be the primary travel expense. Additional costs include local buses or trains to your starting point, which range from €10-€50 depending on the route and starting location.

Miscellaneous Expenses: Extra expenses include laundry (usually €3-€5 per load), entrance fees for some churches or museums, and any gear replacements or souvenirs. Budgeting an extra €5-€10 per day for these extras is a good idea.

Average Daily Budget:

Shoestring Budget: €25-€35 per day, relying on public albergues, basic meals, and occasional grocery store snacks.

Moderate Budget: €40-€60 per day, allowing for a mix of albergues and private rooms, restaurant meals, and some comfort items.

Comfortable Budget: €70+ per day, including private rooms, higher-quality meals, and more flexibility with transportation and activities.

While everyone's budget varies, a moderate budget offers a balance between comfort and affordability, allowing you to enjoy the Camino experience without overspending.

Can I Walk the Camino with Pets?

While walking the Camino with pets, particularly dogs, is possible, it requires extra planning and consideration. Here's what you need to know if you're thinking about bringing your furry friend:

Dog-Friendly Albergues: Not all albergues allow pets, and those that do often have limited spaces. There are some private albergues and hotels that accept dogs, especially on the Camino Francés, but it's essential to call ahead and confirm.

Pet-Friendly Routes: The Camino Francés is generally the most accommodating for pets, as it has more infrastructure and options for dog-friendly accommodations. Routes like the Camino Primitivo and Camino del

Norte, with their remote stretches and limited services, can be challenging for pets due to lack of pet-friendly lodging and tougher terrain.

Vaccination and Health Requirements: If you're bringing a dog from outside the European Union, be aware of vaccination and health certificate requirements for entering Spain. Your pet should be up-to-date on vaccinations, especially rabies. It's also wise to carry a pet first aid kit and know the locations of veterinarians along the route.

Consider the Physical Demands: The Camino's daily distances, varied terrain, and sometimes hot weather can be tough on pets, especially small or older dogs. Dogs will need plenty of water, regular breaks, and a manageable pace to avoid overexertion. It's essential to evaluate whether your pet is fit and healthy enough to handle the physical demands of the Camino.

Pet Supplies and Food: Finding pet food can be hit-or-miss in rural areas along the Camino. It's a good idea to carry a small supply of food and replenish it when passing through larger towns. Consider bringing collapsible water and food bowls, which are easy to pack and can be used on the go.

Respecting Other Pilgrims: While many pilgrims enjoy the company of dogs, others may not feel comfortable around them. Being mindful of your pet's behavior, especially in shared spaces like albergues or crowded trails, is essential to ensure a positive experience for everyone.

Walking the Camino with a pet can be a rewarding experience, providing companionship and adding a unique element to your journey. However, it does require added preparation and flexibility, as not all accommodations and services cater to pets. Be prepared for some logistical challenges, and remember to consider your pet's well-being at every stage of the Camino.

These frequently asked questions address some of the most common concerns and curiosities for pilgrims preparing to walk the Camino. From solo travelers to those bringing pets, understanding the logistics, safety, and practicalities of the Camino ensures that you're well-equipped to embark on this transformative journey. Taking the time to prepare answers to these questions not only reduces stress but also allows you to fully enjoy every step of the Camino de Santiago.

What Should I Do If I Get Injured on the Camino?

Injuries, while not uncommon, can usually be managed with some planning and preparation. Blisters, muscle strain, and knee pain are among the most common ailments pilgrims face. Here's a rundown on how to handle injuries and what resources are available if you need medical assistance:

Basic First Aid: Carry a small first aid kit with essentials like blister pads, antiseptic cream, pain relievers, and bandages. Many pharmacies along the Camino are well-stocked with items specifically for pilgrims, so you can replenish supplies as needed.

Seeking Medical Help: If you have a more serious injury, larger towns and cities along the Camino route have medical facilities and hospitals. In smaller villages, look for the local pharmacy (farmacia), where pharmacists can often offer helpful advice and basic care.

Resting and Recovery: Don't hesitate to take a rest day if you're injured or feeling particularly sore. Many pilgrims feel pressure to keep moving, but allowing yourself to recover can make the difference between a quick recovery and a worsening injury.

Consider Travel Insurance with Medical Coverage: As mentioned earlier, travel insurance that covers medical expenses can be a huge relief in case you need urgent care, X-rays, or other medical attention. Having insurance means you won't have to worry about the cost of getting proper treatment.

Most minor injuries are manageable, and if you listen to your body, you can avoid serious complications. The Camino community is very supportive, and you may even find fellow pilgrims willing to share advice and resources.

How Do I Stay Connected on the Camino?

Staying in touch with loved ones and accessing online resources can be important on the Camino, especially if you're traveling solo or keeping a travel journal. Here are some tips for staying connected:

Wi-Fi Availability: Most albergues and hostels offer free Wi-Fi, especially in larger towns. However, Wi-Fi strength and reliability can vary, so don't rely on it for major uploads or downloads. Many cafes along the route also provide free Wi-Fi if you're a customer.

SIM Cards and Data Plans: If you want more reliable access to data, consider buying a Spanish SIM card. Companies like Vodafone, Orange, and Movistar offer prepaid SIM cards with data plans. This can be particularly useful for navigation apps and keeping in touch without relying on Wi-Fi. Just ensure your phone is unlocked before you go.

Portable Chargers: Charging outlets can be in high demand in shared accommodations, so a portable charger is invaluable. These chargers allow you to keep your phone and other electronics powered up while on the move or when outlets are limited.

Use Social Media to Stay in Touch: Many pilgrims find it rewarding to share updates on social media. Platforms like Instagram and Facebook can be a great way to stay connected with friends and family and let them follow your journey.

Staying connected allows you to share experiences, seek advice, and reach out in case of emergencies. With the right setup, you can stay in touch while still embracing the Camino's opportunity to unplug and enjoy the journey.

What Kind of Physical Preparation is Needed for the Camino?

While the Camino is accessible to many fitness levels, physical preparation will make the journey much more enjoyable. Here's how to get yourself Camino-ready:

Build Up Walking Endurance: The best way to prepare is by walking, ideally with a loaded backpack. Start with shorter distances and gradually increase to the average 15-25 kilometers (9-15 miles) you'll cover daily on the Camino. Practice walking on different terrains and elevations to mimic the varied Camino paths.

Strengthen Core and Leg Muscles: Focus on exercises that strengthen your legs, core, and lower back. Squats, lunges, and planks are excellent for building endurance and stability, which help prevent injuries.

Get Used to Your Gear: Break in your hiking boots well before departure. Walk with your backpack loaded to get used to the weight, adjusting the straps for comfort. This practice will help you avoid blisters, sore shoulders, and other gear-related issues.

Plan for Rest Days: Build a training schedule that includes rest days, mirroring the breaks you might take on the Camino itself. This teaches your body to handle consecutive days of walking, with periodic rests to recover.

Preparing physically for the Camino can significantly reduce the risk of injuries and ensure you have the stamina needed for a smooth journey. With the right preparation, you'll be able to focus on the experience rather than physical discomfort.

What's the Best Time of Year to Walk the Camino?

Choosing the right time of year to walk the Camino is crucial, as it affects everything from weather conditions to crowd sizes and accommodation availability. Here's a breakdown of each season's pros and cons:

Spring (April to June):

Pros: Mild temperatures, blooming landscapes, and fewer crowds than peak summer months.

Cons: Rain can be frequent, especially in northern Spain. Early spring can be chilly, particularly in the mountainous sections.

Summer (July and August):

Pros: Warm weather, long daylight hours, and most services are open.

Cons: Crowds are at their peak, making it harder to secure accommodations without reservations.

The heat, especially on the Meseta, can be intense.

Fall (September and October):

Pros: Cooler temperatures, beautiful autumn colors, and smaller crowds than summer.

Cons: Shorter days and the risk of rain increases as October approaches. Some accommodations start to close for the season in late October.

Winter (November to March):

Pros: Few crowds, quiet trails, and a sense of solitude.

Cons: Many albergues are closed, especially on the Camino Francés. Cold temperatures, snow, and rain are common, making certain paths, like the Camino Primitivo, particularly challenging.

Most pilgrims find spring and fall to be the ideal balance between weather, crowd levels, and accommodation availability. Choosing the right season depends on your tolerance for weather conditions and whether you prefer a lively or more solitary Camino experience.

How Should I Handle Language Barriers?

While many people speak basic English along the Camino, especially in larger towns, learning a few Spanish phrases goes a long way. Here are some tips for navigating language differences:

Learn Basic Spanish Phrases: Knowing essentials like "Where is...?" (¿Dónde está...?), "How much does it cost?" (¿Cuánto cuesta?), and "Thank you" (Gracias) makes a difference. A friendly attitude combined with a few Spanish phrases usually earns positive responses from locals.

Use a Translation App: Apps like Google Translate can be helpful, especially if you download the Spanish language pack for offline use. You can use the camera function for menus or signs, which is convenient in rural areas where English translations may not be available.

Body Language: Simple gestures can bridge language gaps. Pointing, miming, and nodding are universal and can help you communicate basic needs even if words fail.

Seek Out English-Speaking Pilgrims or Staff: Some albergues and cafes along the Camino employ English-speaking staff, particularly in popular areas. Fellow pilgrims are often happy to help translate, as well.

Learning a bit of Spanish not only helps with logistics but also enhances your cultural experience on the Camino. Locals appreciate the effort, and even basic Spanish can open doors to friendly conversations and shared stories.

The Camino de Santiago is full of both expected and unexpected moments, from the thrill of setting out on the first day to the satisfaction of reaching Santiago de Compostela. These frequently asked questions help address common concerns, so you can start your journey with a clear sense of what to expect, and a toolkit of knowledge that will empower you to fully embrace everything the Camino has to offer. With a bit of preparation, a flexible attitude, and a sense of adventure, the Camino becomes not just a path to a destination, but an unforgettable life experience filled with self-discovery, camaraderie, and a deep connection to history and tradition.

Made in the USA
Coppell, TX
30 December 2024

43730378R00098